Comfort
food

The Confident Cooking Promise of Success

Welcome to the world of Confident Cooking,
where recipes are double-tested by our team
of home economists to achieve a high standard
of success—and delicious results every time.

bay books

C O N T E

Lemon delicious, page 97

Chicken curry, page 30

Cauliflower cheese, page 66

Beef pie, page 24

Chicken and corn soup, page 49

Sticky date pudding, page 87

The Publisher thanks the following for their assistance: Chief Australia, Sunbeam Corporation, Kambrook, Sheldon & Hammond, Southcorp Appliances, Bertoli Olive Oil, Dinosaur Designs, Style Lamination and The Bay Tree.

All recipes are double-tested by our team of home economists. When we test our recipes, we rate them for ease of preparation. The following cookery ratings are on the recipes in this book, making them easy to use and understand.

A single Cooking with Confidence symbol indicates a recipe that is simple and generally quick to make—perfect for beginners.

Two symbols indicate the need for just a little more care and a little more time.

Three symbols indicate special dishes that need more investment in time, care and patience—but the results are worth it.

IMPORTANT

Those who might be at risk from the effects of salmonella food poisoning (the elderly, pregnant women, young children and those suffering from immune deficiency diseases) should consult their doctor with any concerns about eating raw eggs.

Leek and prosciutto risotto, page 10

Roast chicken, page 43

HEARTY HELPINGS

CHICKEN AND LEEK PIE

Preparation time: 20 minutes
Total cooking time: 40 minutes
Serves 4

50 g (1³/4 oz) butter
2 large leeks, washed and
    finely sliced
4 spring onions (scallions),
    sliced
1 garlic clove, crushed
30 g (¹/4 cup) plain (all-purpose)
    flour
375 ml (1¹/2 cups) chicken stock
125 ml (¹/2 cup) cream
1 medium barbecued chicken,
    chopped
2 sheets puff pastry, thawed
60 ml (¹/4 cup) milk

1 Preheat the oven to 200°C (400°F/Gas 6). In a frying pan, melt the butter and add the leek, spring onion and garlic. Cook over low heat for 6 minutes, or until the leek is soft but not browned. Sprinkle in the flour and mix well. Pour in the stock gradually and cook, stirring, until the mixture is thick and smooth.
2 Stir in the cream and add the chicken. Put the mixture in a shallow 20 cm (8 inch) pie dish and set aside to cool.
3 Cut a circle out of one of the sheets of pastry to cover the top of the pie. Paint around the rim of the pie dish with a little milk. Put the pastry on top and seal around the edge firmly. Trim off any overhanging pastry and decorate the edge with the back of a fork. Cut the other sheet into thin strips and roll each strip up loosely like a snail. Arrange the spirals on top of the pie, starting from the middle and leaving a gap between each one. The spirals may not cover the whole surface of the pie. Make a few small holes between the spirals to let out any steam, and brush the top of the pie lightly with milk.
4 Cook in the oven for 25–30 minutes, or until the top is brown and crispy. Make sure the spirals look well cooked and are not raw in the middle. Serve with a fresh garden salad.

NUTRITION PER SERVE
Protein 25 g; Fat 55 g; Carbohydrate 40 g;
Dietary Fibre 3 g; Cholesterol 185 mg;
3105 kJ (740 Cal)

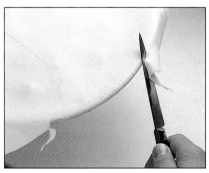

Seal the edge firmly and trim off any overhanging pastry with a sharp knife.

Roll up the strips of pastry like a snail and arrange them on top of the pie.

MEAT LOAF

Preparation time: 25 minutes
Total cooking time: 1 hour 15 minutes
Serves 6

125 g (4½ oz) streaky bacon,
   trimmed and chopped
500 g (1 lb 2 oz) minced
   (ground) beef
500 g (1 lb 2 oz) minced
   (ground) pork
1 onion, coarsely grated
2 garlic cloves, crushed
160 g (2 cups) fresh
   breadcrumbs
2 teaspoons thyme leaves
1 egg, lightly beaten
1 tablespoon red wine vinegar
2 teaspoons soft brown sugar

1 Preheat the oven to 180°C (350°F/ Gas 4). Lightly grease a loaf tin then line with a single sheet of baking paper, leaving the paper to overhang on the long sides of the tin.

2 Heat a non-stick frying pan, add the bacon, and cook, stirring, until crispy. Drain on paper towels.

3 Place the meat, onion, garlic, breadcrumbs, thyme, egg, vinegar, sugar and bacon in a large bowl. Season and mix together using your hands. Don't overmix or the meat loaf will become too dense when it is cooked.

4 Spoon the mixture into the tin and press down gently. Smooth the top and bake for 1 hour 10 minutes, or until browned and cooked through. Test if it is cooked by pushing a metal skewer or sharp knife into the centre, leaving it for 3 seconds, and then pulling it out and holding it against your wrist. If it is really hot, it is cooked through; if not, cook a little longer. Leave for 5 minutes and pour the cooking juices into a jug. Lift out the meat loaf using the overhanging baking paper. Cut into slices with a serrated knife and drizzle with the cooking juices. Serve with tomato sauce, peas, corn and potatoes.

NUTRITION PER SERVE
Protein 45 g; Fat 13 g; Carbohydrate 20 g; Dietary Fibre 1.5 g; Cholesterol 135 mg; 1588 kJ (380 Cal)

Line the tin with baking paper, allowing it to overhang the long sides of the tin.

Spoon the mixture into the tin and gently press down with the back of a spoon.

LAMB'S LIVER AND BACON

Preparation time: 10 minutes
Total cooking time: 10 minutes
Serves 4

500 g (1 lb 2 oz) lamb's liver
1 tablespoon olive oil
1 large onion, sliced
125 g (4¹/2 oz) streaky bacon,
    cut into strips
30 g (1 oz) butter
1 tablespoon plain (all-purpose)
    flour
300 ml (10 fl oz) beef stock
2 tablespoons chopped parsley

1 Remove the membrane and tubes from the liver and slice horizontally into thin slices.
2 Heat the oil in a large non-stick frying pan and cook the onion and bacon until browned. Remove from the pan and keep warm.
3 Turn up the heat and add the butter to the frying pan until it sizzles. Quickly cook the liver in batches over high heat for about 1 minute on each side. Do not overcook the liver or it will become tough. Return all the liver to the pan with the bacon and onion. Sprinkle the flour over the top and toss to coat. Gradually add the stock and stir until the sauce boils and thickens. Season to taste. Stir in the parsley and serve immediately with fried tomato slices and mashed potato.

NUTRITION PER SERVE
Protein 35 g; Fat 22 g; Carbohydrate 7 g;
Dietary Fibre 0.5 g; Cholesterol 578 mg;
1526 kJ (364 Cal)

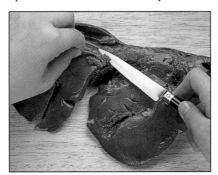
Remove the membrane and tubes from the liver with a small sharp knife.

Quickly cook the liver slices in batches over high heat.

SAUSAGES AND MASH WITH ONION GRAVY

Preparation time: 10 minutes
Total cooking time: 50 minutes
Serves 4

375 ml (1½ cups) beef stock
2 teaspoons cornflour
    (cornstarch)
2 teaspoons balsamic vinegar
1 tablespoon oil
6 onions, sliced
1.5 kg (3 lb 5 oz) potatoes,
    chopped
60 g (2¼ oz) butter
125 ml (½ cup) cream
8 beef sausages

1 Mix together 1 tablespoon stock with the cornflour, and stir to dissolve, ensuring there are no lumps. Add to the remaining stock with the vinegar.
2 To make the onion gravy, heat the oil in a large frying pan, add the onion and cook over low heat for 35–40 minutes, or until the onion is soft and beginning to caramelize. Increase the heat and slowly add the stock mixture, stirring constantly until the mixture thickens. Remove from the heat and set aside.
3 Meanwhile, put the potatoes in a large pan of boiling water and cook for 15–20 minutes, or until tender. Drain the potatoes and return them to the pan with the butter and cream. With a potato masher, mash until smooth and creamy. Season to taste with salt and black pepper.
4 Prick the sausages and cook under a hot grill (broiler), turning once, for 10 minutes, or until cooked through.
5 Gently warm the gravy and serve with sausages and mashed potato. Delicious with baked zucchini.

NUTRITION PER SERVE
Protein 30 g; Fat 70 g; Carbohydrate 63 g; Dietary Fibre 13 g; Cholesterol 160 mg; 4280 kJ (1025 Cal)

Cook the onion in the oil until soft and beginning to caramelize.

Slowly pour in the stock mixture and stir constantly until the gravy thickens.

RISOTTO

Preparation time: 5 minutes
Total cooking time: 40 minutes
Serves 4

1.25 litres (5 cups) chicken stock
250 ml (1 cup) dry white wine
2 tablespoons extra virgin olive
  oil
30 g (1 oz) butter
1 large onion, finely chopped
330 g (1½ cups) arborio rice
100 g (1 cup) grated Parmesan
  cheese, plus extra, to serve
rosemary, to serve

1 Pour the stock and wine into a pan and slowly bring to the boil, then reduce the heat and keep the stock at simmering point. In a large, heavy-based pan, heat 1 tablespoon of olive oil and butter. When the butter is melted, add the onion and cook over low heat until the onion is soft but not brown. Add the rice and stir using a wooden spoon for 1 minute, or until the rice is coated in the butter.
2 Add a ladleful of hot stock to the rice and stir over low heat until the stock is completely absorbed by the rice. Repeat this process several times until the rice is tender and creamy. (This will take 25–30 minutes and you may not need to use all the stock.) The rice should be just tender, or resist slightly when bitten, but not chalky.
3 Remove the pan from the heat and stir in the Parmesan and remaining oil. Serve immediately. Garnish with rosemary and extra Parmesan.

NUTRITION PER SERVE
Protein 20 g; Fat 30 g; Carbohydrate 90 g; Dietary Fibre 3 g; Cholesterol 55 mg; 3296 kJ (785 Cal)

COOK'S FILE

Note: Don't wash the arborio rice, as the starch released during cooking binds the ingredients together.
Variation: For a tasty variation, add any of the following ingredients to the risotto in the last 5 minutes of cooking.

● chopped rocket (arugula) leaves and walnuts
● chopped raw prawns (shrimps) and chives
● cooked and chopped asparagus

Add the rice to the pan and stir to coat with the butter.

Pour a ladleful of hot stock into the pan with the rice.

Stir over low heat until the stock has been completely absorbed into the rice.

LEEK AND PROSCIUTTO RISOTTO WITH PARSLEY PISTOU

Preparation time: 10 minutes
Total cooking time: 45 minutes
Serves 2

Parsley pistou
60 ml (1/4 cup) extra virgin olive oil
1 garlic clove, crushed
2 tablespoons chopped flat-leaf (Italian) parsley

100 g (3 1/2 oz) prosciutto
750 ml (3 cups) chicken stock
60 g (2 1/4 oz) butter
2 leeks, halved lengthways and sliced
1 celery stalk, sliced thinly
440 g (2 cups) arborio rice

125 ml (1/2 cup) dry white wine
2 teaspoons thyme

1 To make the pistou, combine the oil, garlic, parsley and 1/2 teaspoon cracked pepper in a blender or mortar and pestle and blend until combined.

2 Place the prosciutto on an oven tray lined with foil and cook under a hot grill (broiler) for 3 minutes, or until crisp. Allow to cool, then break into small pieces.

3 Put the stock and 750 ml (3 cups) water in a pan, bring to the boil, then reduce the heat to simmering.

4 Heat the butter over medium heat in a large heavy-based pan. When foaming, add the leek and cook, stirring occasionally, for 7 minutes, or until soft. Add the celery and rice and stir for 1 minute, or until the rice is coated in the butter. Add the wine, allow it to boil until almost dry, then add 125 ml (1/2 cup) of the hot stock and stir over low heat with a wooden spoon until all the liquid is absorbed. Continue adding the stock a ladleful at a time, stirring continuously until it is completely absorbed before the next addition. The risotto will be ready after 20–25 minutes when the rice grains are swollen and the mixture appears creamy. You may not need to use all the stock. The rice should be just tender, or resist slightly when bitten, but not chalky. Stir through the prosciutto, thyme and season to taste with salt. Spoon into serving bowls and swirl through some of the parsley pistou. Serve immediately.

NUTRITION PER SERVE
Protein 15 g; Fat 55 g; Carbohydrate 175 g; Dietary Fibre 7 g; Cholesterol 75 mg; 5465 kJ (1305 Cal)

Stir in the celery and rice until the rice is coated in butter.

Add the wine and allow the mixture to boil until almost dry.

Pour in a ladleful of stock and stir until completely absorbed.

SALMON AND BASIL FISHCAKES

Preparation time: 20 minutes + chilling
Total cooking time: 25 minutes
Serves 4

400 g (14 oz) desiree potatoes,
    quartered
415 g (14¹/2 oz) can pink
    salmon, drained, skin and
    large bones removed
¹/2 teaspoon grated lime zest
4 spring onions (scallions),
    finely chopped
15 g (¹/4 cup) roughly chopped
    basil leaves
1 tablespoon capers, rinsed,
    drained, roughly chopped
1 egg yolk
1 egg, lightly beaten
1 tablespoon milk
40 g (¹/3 cup) plain (all-purpose)
    flour
75 g (³/4 cup) dry breadcrumbs
oil, for pan-frying

1 Cook the potatoes in a large pan of boiling water until just tender.

Drain and lightly mash, leaving some large pieces. Allow to cool.
2 Meanwhile, in a bowl, gently flake the salmon into large pieces. Add the lime zest, spring onion, basil, capers, and egg yolk. Mix lightly and season to taste with salt and pepper. Stir in the potato.
3 Combine the egg and milk in a shallow bowl. Spread the flour and breadcrumbs out on separate plates. Shape the salmon mixture into eight patties about 6 cm (2¹/2 inches) in diameter, pressing the mixture firmly together. Dust with flour, and shake off any excess. Dip the fishcakes into

the egg mixture, then coat in the breadcrumbs. Place the patties on a tray, and refrigerate, covered, for 30 minutes, or until firm.
4 Add enough oil to come one third of the way up a large deep frying pan. Heat over high heat. Cook the patties for 3–4 minutes each side, or until golden and heated through. Drain on paper towels. Serve with mashed sweet potato and minted peas.

NUTRITION PER SERVE
Protein 30 g; Fat 30 g; Carbohydrate 35 g; Dietary Fibre 3 g; Cholesterol 155 mg; 2170 kJ (520 Cal)

Dust the fishcakes with flour then shake off any excess.

Dip the patties in the egg mixture and coat in the breadcrumbs.

FISH PIE

Preparation time: 10 minutes
Total cooking time: 45 minutes
Serves 4

2 large potatoes, chopped
60 ml (1/4 cup) milk or cream
1 egg
60 g (2 1/4 oz) butter
60 g (1/2 cup) grated cheese
800 g (1 lb 12 oz) white fish
    fillets, cut into large chunks
375 ml (1 1/2 cups) milk
1 onion, finely chopped
1 garlic clove, crushed
2 tablespoons plain (all-purpose)
    flour

2 tablespoons lemon juice
2 teaspoons lemon zest
1 tablespoon chopped dill

1 Preheat the oven to 180°C (350°F/ Gas 4). Boil the potatoes until tender. Drain and mash well with the milk or cream, egg and half the butter. Mix in half the cheese, then set aside and keep warm.

2 Put the fish in a shallow frying pan and cover with the milk. Bring to the boil, then reduce the heat and simmer for 2–3 minutes, or until the fish flakes when tested with a knife. Drain the fish well, reserving the milk, and set aside.

3 Melt the remaining butter over medium heat in a pan and cook the onion and garlic for 2 minutes. Stir in the flour and cook for 1 minute, or until pale and foaming. Remove from the heat and gradually stir in the reserved milk. Return to the heat and stir constantly until the sauce boils and thickens. Reduce the heat and simmer for 2 minutes. Add the lemon juice, lemon zest and dill, and season.

4 Put the fish into a 1.5 litre (6 cup) ovenproof dish and gently mix in the sauce. Spoon the potato over the fish and top with the remaining cheese. Bake in the oven for 35 minutes.

NUTRITION PER SERVE
Protein 55 g; Fat 30 g; Carbohydrate 25 g; Dietary Fibre 3 g; Cholesterol 255 mg; 2460 kJ (585 Cal)

Use a potato masher to mash the potatoes with the milk or cream, egg and butter.

Put the pieces of fish in a frying pan and cover with the milk.

Put spoonfuls of the potato mixture on top of the fish.

TUNA MORNAY

Preparation time: 20 minutes
Total cooking time: 25 minutes
Serves 4

60 g (2 1/4 oz) butter
2 tablespoons plain (all-purpose)
    flour
500 ml (2 cups) milk
1/2 teaspoon dry mustard
90 g (3/4 cup) grated cheese
600 g (1 lb 5 oz) tin tuna in
    brine, drained
2 tablespoons chopped parsley
2 hard boiled eggs, chopped
25 g (1/3 cup) breadcrumbs
paprika, to season

1 Preheat the oven to 180°C (350°F/ Gas 4). Melt the butter in a pan, then add the flour and stir over low heat for 1 minute. Remove the pan from the heat and add the milk gradually, stirring until smooth between each addition.

2 Return the pan to the heat and stir constantly until the sauce boils and thickens. Reduce the heat and simmer for 2 minutes. Remove from the heat, whisk in the mustard and 60 g (1/2 cup) cheese until smooth.

3 Flake the tuna with a fork, and mix into the sauce. Add the parsley and egg and season with salt and pepper.

Spoon the mixture into four 250 ml (1 cup) ramekins. Mix together the breadcrumbs and remaining cheese and sprinkle over the mornay. Dust with paprika. Bake for 15–20 minutes, or until topping is golden brown.

NUTRITION PER SERVE
Protein 55 g; Fat 30 g; Carbohydrate 15 g; Dietary Fibre 0.5 g; Cholesterol 260 mg; 2320 kJ (555 Cal)

Gradually add the milk, stirring until smooth between each addition.

Use a fork to flake the tuna, then stir it into the sauce.

*Fish pie (top)
and Tuna mornay*

LASAGNE

Preparation time: 25 minutes
Total cooking time: 1 hour
Serves 6

Meat sauce
1 tablespoon olive oil
750 g (1 lb 10 oz) minced
 (ground) beef
1 onion, finely chopped
2 finely chopped celery stalks
400 g (14 oz) can chopped
 tomatoes
2 tablespoons tomato paste
 (purée)
1 teaspoon dried mixed herbs
1–2 teaspoons sugar

Bechamel sauce
60 g (2¼ oz) butter
3 tablespoons plain (all-purpose)
 flour
750 ml (3 cups) milk

375 g (13 oz) fresh lasagne
 sheets
125 g (1 cup) grated Cheddar
 cheese

1 Preheat the oven to 180°C (350°F/ Gas 4). Heat half the oil in a large pan and brown the meat in batches. Remove from the pan. Add the remaining oil and cook the onion and celery until soft. Return the meat to the pan and add all other ingredients. Bring to the boil, then reduce the heat and simmer, covered, for 20 minutes.
2 Melt the butter in a pan over low heat. Stir in the flour and cook for 1 minute. Remove from the heat and gradually stir in the milk. Return to the heat and stir constantly until the sauce boils and thickens. Reduce the heat and simmer for 2 minutes.
3 Lightly brush a 2.5 litre (10 cup) ovenproof dish with oil. Spoon one third of the meat sauce into the dish. Top with a single layer of the lasagne sheets, then spoon on one third of the bechamel sauce. Repeat layering twice more, and top with Cheddar.
4 Bake in the oven for 25 minutes, or until golden and heated through.

NUTRITION PER SERVE
Protein 45 g; Fat 40 g; Carbohydrate 60 g; Dietary Fibre 5 g; Cholesterol 140 mg; 3131 kJ (780 Cal)

Peel and finely chop the onion with a large sharp knife.

Mix in the meat, tomatoes, tomato paste, dried herbs and sugar.

Slowly add the milk and stir constantly until the sauce begins to thicken.

Spoon some of the bechamel sauce over the lasagne sheets.

SPAGHETTI WITH MEATBALLS

Preparation time: 40 minutes
Total cooking time: 30 minutes
Serves 4

Meatballs
500 g (1 lb 2 oz) minced
    (ground) beef
40 g (1/2 cup) breadcrumbs
1 onion, finely chopped
2 garlic cloves, crushed
2 teaspoons Worcestershire
    sauce
1 teaspoon dried oregano
30 g (1/4 cup) plain (all-purpose)
    flour
2 tablespoons olive oil

Sauce
2 x 400 g (14 oz) cans chopped
    tomatoes
1 tablespoon olive oil
1 onion, finely chopped
2 garlic cloves, crushed
2 tablespoons tomato paste
    (purée)
125 ml (1/2 cup) beef stock
2 teaspoons sugar

500 g (1 lb 2 oz) spaghetti
grated Parmesan cheese,
    to serve

1 Put the meat, breadcrumbs, onion, garlic, Worcestershire sauce and oregano in a bowl and season. Mix together with your hands. Roll tablespoons of the mixt into balls, dust lightly with the flour and shake off the excess. Heat the oil in a deep frying pan and cook the balls in batches, turning, until evenly browned. Drain well.
2 To make the sauce, purée the tomatoes in a food processor. Heat the oil in a frying pan. Add the onion and cook over medium heat for a few

minutes until soft. Add the garlic and cook for 1 minute more. Add the puréed tomatoes, tomato paste, stock and sugar to the pan and stir well. Bring the mixture to the boil, and add the meatballs. Reduce the heat and simmer for 15 minutes, turning the meatballs once.
3 Meanwhile, cook the spaghetti in a large pan of boiling water until just tender. Drain, divide among serving bowls and top with the meatballs and sauce. Serve with Parmesan.

NUTRITION PER SERVE
Protein 45 g; Fat 30 g; Carbohydrate 112 g;
Dietary Fibre 11 g; Cholesterol 85 mg;
3875 kJ (925 Cal)

With clean hands, roll the mixture into balls and dust with flour.

Cook the meatballs in batches, turning frequently, until browned all over.

SILVERSIDE AND PARSLEY SAUCE

Preparation time: 20 minutes + soaking
Total cooking time: 2 hours
Serves 6

1.5 kg (3 lb 5 oz) corned beef
1 teaspoon black peppercorns
5 whole cloves
2 bay leaves, torn
2 tablespoons soft brown sugar

Parsley sauce
50 g (1¾ oz) butter
1½ tablespoons plain
  (all-purpose) flour
400 ml (14 fl oz) milk
125 ml (½ cup) beef stock
2 tablespoons chopped parsley

1 Soak the corned beef in cold water for 45 minutes, changing the water 3–4 times. This helps eliminate some of the salty flavour.

2 Remove the beef from the water and place in a large saucepan with the peppercorns, cloves, bay leaves, brown sugar and enough cold water to just cover. Bring to the boil, then reduce the heat to very low and simmer for 1½–1¾ hours. Turn the meat over every 30 minutes and add more water when needed. Do not let the water boil or the beef will be tough. Remove from the pan, wrap in foil and leave to stand for at least 15 minutes before carving.

3 To make the parsley sauce, melt the butter in a pan over medium heat, and stir in the flour. Cook, stirring with a wooden spoon, for 1 minute.

Take the pan off the heat and pour in the milk and stock, whisking until smooth. Return the pan to the heat and cook, whisking constantly, until the sauce boils and thickens. Reduce the heat and simmer for 2 minutes more. Stir in the parsley and season with salt and pepper.

4 To serve, slice the meat across the grain and arrange on warmed plates. Spoon on a little of the sauce and serve the remaining sauce in a jug. Accompany with large florets of cauliflower, whole peeled baby carrots and wedges of cabbage (the vegetables are delicious if you cook them in the meat water).

NUTRITION PER SERVE
Protein 50 g; Fat 15 g; Carbohydrate 10 g; Dietary Fibre 0 g; Cholesterol 100 mg; 1625 kJ (390 Cal)

Soak the corned beef in cold water to help eliminate some of the saltiness.

Put the beef, peppercorns, cloves, bay leaves and sugar in a pan and cover with water.

Make sure you turn the meat every half hour or so.

BEEF CARBONNADE

Preparation time: 15 minutes
Total cooking time: 3 hours 25 minutes
Serves 4

1 leek, green part only
1 bay leaf
1 fresh thyme sprig
1 sprig celery leaves
4 fresh parsley sprigs
2 tablespoons butter
1 tablespoon oil
1 kg (2 lb 4 oz) chuck or
    stewing steak, cubed
2 onions, sliced
2 garlic cloves, crushed
2 tablespoons plain (all-purpose)
    flour
375 ml (1¹/₂ cups) brown ale
1 baguette
¹/₂ tablespoon French mustard
¹/₂ tablespoon butter, softened

1 To make a bouquet garni, wrap the green part of the leek loosely around the bay leaf, thyme sprig, celery leaves and parsley, then tie together with string. Leave a long tail to the string for easy removal.

2 Preheat the oven to 180°C (350°F/ Gas 4). Heat the butter and oil in a large pan and cook the beef in batches for 3–4 minutes, or until well browned. Remove from the pan. Lower the heat and cook the onion and garlic until translucent. Sprinkle in the flour, stir well, then cook for 1 minute. Combine the beer with 375 ml (1¹/₂ cups) water and pour into the pan. Stir well, scraping the base of the pan as you go. Bring to the boil and return the meat to the pan. Add the bouquet garni and return to the boil. Transfer to a 2.5 litre (10 cup) casserole dish, cover well with foil and cook in the oven for 2¹/₂ hours.

Leave a long tail of string on the bouquet garni for easy removal.

3 Cut the bread into 2 cm (³/₄ inch) slices and spread with the combined mustard and butter. Remove the casserole from the oven, take out the bouquet garni and skim off any fat. Put the bread on the surface of the casserole, mustard-side-up, and press down gently to cover with juice. Return to the oven and cook, uncovered, for another 30–40 minutes, or until the bread is crusty. Serve with green vegetables.

NUTRITION PER SERVE
Protein 60 g; Fat 25 g; Carbohydrate 30 g; Dietary Fibre 3.5 g; Cholesterol 195 mg; 2455 kJ (585 Cal)

Cook the beef in batches until well browned all over.

BEEF IN RED WINE

Preparation time: 20 minutes
Total cooking time: 2 hours 15 minutes
Serves 4

2 tablespoons olive oil
1 kg (2 lb 4 oz) trimmed chuck
    steak, cubed
12 baby onions, halved, with
    root base left intact
4 rashers back bacon, chopped
2 garlic cloves, finely chopped
3 tablespoons plain (all-purpose)
    flour
375 ml (1½ cups) red wine
2 tablespoons port
2 bay leaves
5 fresh parsley sprigs
3 fresh thyme sprigs
1 thin slice lemon zest
375 ml (1½ cups) beef stock
500 g (1 lb 2 oz) flat
    mushrooms, halved

1 Heat 1 tablespoon of oil in a large frying pan, and cook the steak in small batches over high heat for 2 minutes, or until well browned. Remove from the pan.

2 Heat the remaining oil in the same pan, and add the onion, bacon and garlic. Stir over high heat for 5 minutes, or until the onion is browned. Return the beef to the pan, add the flour, and stir for 1 minute. Remove the pan from the heat, and gradually stir in the wine and port, mixing the flour in well. Return the pan to the heat and bring to the boil, stirring, then reduce the heat and simmer for 3 minutes, or until the sauce boils and thickens slightly.

3 Wrap the bay leaves, parsley, thyme and lemon zest in a piece of muslin and tie with string. Add the bouquet garni, stock and mushrooms to the pan, bring to the boil, then reduce the heat to low and simmer, covered, for 2 hours, or until the beef is tender, stirring occasionally. Remove the bouquet garni, and season to taste with salt and pepper. Serve with mashed potato and baby carrots.

NUTRITION PER SERVE
Protein 65 g; Fat 20 g; Carbohydrate 12 g; Dietary Fibre 4.5 g; Cholesterol 185 mg; 2332 kJ (557 Cal)

Chop the baby onions in half, leaving the root base intact.

Cook the steak in batches until well browned all over.

Gradually add the wine and port, and stir to mix in the flour.

BEEF POT ROAST

Preparation time: 15 minutes
Total cooking time: 3 hours 15 minutes
Serves 6

300 g (10½ oz) pickling onions
2 carrots
3 parsnips, peeled
40 g (1½ oz) butter
1.5 kg (3 lb 5 oz) piece of
    silverside, trimmed of fat
60 ml (¼ cup) dry red wine
1 large tomato, finely chopped
250 ml (1 cup) beef stock

1 Put the onions in a heatproof bowl and cover with boiling water. Leave for 1 minute, then drain well. Allow to cool then peel off the skins.
2 Cut the carrots and parsnips in half lengthways then into even-sized pieces. Heat half the butter in a large saucepan that will tightly fit the meat (it will shrink during cooking), add the onions, carrot and parsnip and cook, stirring, over high heat until browned. Remove from the pan. Add the remaining butter to the pan and add the meat, browning well all over. Increase the heat to high and pour in the wine. Bring to the boil, then add the tomato and stock. Return to the boil, then reduce the heat to low, cover and simmer for 2 hours, turning once. Add the vegetables and simmer, covered, for 1 hour.

3 Remove the meat from the pan and put it on a board ready for carving. Cover with foil and leave it to stand while finishing the sauce.
4 Increase the heat to high and boil the pan juices with the vegetables for 10 minutes to reduce and thicken slightly. Skim off any excess fat, and season to taste. Slice the meat and arrange on a serving platter or individual serving plates with the vegetables. Drizzle generously with the pan juices. Serve with mustard on the side.

NUTRITION PER SERVE
Protein 60 g; Fat 10 g; Carbohydrate 95 g; Dietary Fibre 3.5 g; Cholesterol 185 mg; 1690 kJ (405 Cal)

Put the pickling onions in a bowl and cover with boiling water.

Add the meat to the pan and brown well on all sides.

Put the vegetables in with the meat, then cover and simmer for 1 hour.

Purées and mashes

The success story of the humble mashed potato takes on a new twist with these delicious purées and mashes. Nutritious and simple to make, they are perfect for soaking up the juices of casseroles or as an accompaniment to lamb chops or juicy steaks. All side dishes serve four.

CREAMED SPINACH PUREE

Wash and roughly chop 1 kg (2 lb 4 oz) English spinach. Heat 60 g ($2^1/4$ oz) butter in a saucepan and cook the spinach over high heat until it is wilted and the liquid has evaporated. Put in a food processor or blender with 120 ml ($^1/2$ cup) cream and process until smooth. Season to taste with salt, pepper and nutmeg. Makes about 500 g (2 cups).

NUTRITION PER SERVE
Protein 6 g; Fat 26 g; Carbohydrate 2 g; Dietary Fibre 8 g; Cholesterol 80 mg; 1114 kJ (266 Cal)

PEA PUREE

Melt 50 g ($1^3/4$ oz) butter in a pan over low heat and add 2 crushed garlic cloves. Stir briefly and then add 500 g (2 cups) frozen peas. Cover and increase the heat to moderate and, shaking the pan occasionally, cook the peas for 5 minutes, or until tender. Mash roughly until you have a coarse purée. Season well. Makes about 500 g (2 cups).

NUTRITION PER SERVE
Protein 7.5 g; Fat 11 g; Carbohydrate 8 g; Dietary Fibre 8 g; Cholesterol 32 mg; 650 kJ (155 Cal)

From left to right: Creamed spinach purée; Roast pumpkin purée; Very comforting cheesy mash; Pea purée; Beetroot purée; Butterbean and rosemary purée

ROAST PUMPKIN PUREE

Preheat the oven to 200°C (400°F/Gas 6). Remove the seeds from 750 g (1 lb 10 oz) pumpkin and cut into pieces. Put them on an oven tray, brush with olive oil and roast for 35 minutes, or until the pumpkin is tender and the edges are a little blackened. Remove from the tray, cool slightly, then peel off the skin. Place in a food processor or mash with a masher until you have a purée, then add 60 ml (1/4 cup) sour cream. Season well. Makes about 500 g (2 cups).

NUTRITION PER SERVE
Protein 4 g; Fat 9 g; Carbohydrate 13 g; Dietary Fibre 2 g; Cholesterol 20 mg; 623 kJ (149 cal)

VERY COMFORTING CHEESY MASH

Cut 900 g (2 lb) floury potatoes into chunks. Place them in a pan of water and boil for 20 minutes. Drain and transfer to a bowl. Add 2 crushed garlic cloves and 80 ml (1/3 cup) cream, and mash, then beat until fluffy. Season well. Stir in 300 g (10 1/2 oz) grated cheese and beat until the cheese is melted. Season to taste. Makes 500 g (1 1/2 cups).

NUTRITION PER SERVE
Protein 25 g; Fat 34 g; Carbohydrate 30 g; Dietary Fibre 4 g; Cholesterol 102 mg; 2220 kJ (530 cal)

BEETROOT PUREE

Preheat the oven to 180°C (350°F/Gas 4). Wrap 500 g (1 lb 2 oz) unpeeled beetroot in foil and bake for 50 minutes, or until they are soft to the touch. Cool, then peel off the skin and cut into pieces. Fry 1 chopped onion in 1 tablespoon olive oil until soft but not browned. Add the beetroot and 1 tablespoon balsamic vinegar and stir until heated through. Mash with a masher, then stir in 2 tablespoons cream. Makes 500 g (2 cups).

NUTRITION PER SERVE
Protein 3 g; Fat 9 g; Carbohydrate 12 g; Dietary Fibre 4 g; Cholesterol 14 mg; 592 kJ (142 cal)

BUTTERBEAN AND ROSEMARY PUREE

Heat 2 tablespoons olive oil in a pan over a low heat and add 2 crushed garlic cloves. Stir briefly until softened, then add 1.2 kg (2 lb 12 oz) tins drained butter (lima) beans and 2 tablespoons chopped rosemary and cook until heated through. Season well, then mash roughly with 2–4 tablespoons olive oil, until smooth. Drizzle with extra olive oil if desired. Makes about 375 g (1 1/2 cups).

NUTRITION PER SERVE
Protein 4 g; Fat 10 g; Carbohydrate 4 g; Dietary Fibre 6 g; Cholesterol 0 mg; 501 kJ (120 cal)

CHILLI CON CARNE

Preparation time: 25 minutes +
  overnight soaking
Total cooking time: 2 hours 15 minutes
Serves 6

185 g (6¹/2 oz) dried black eye
  beans
650 g (1 lb 7 oz) tomatoes
1¹/2 tablespoons oil
900 g (2 lb) trimmed chuck
  steak, cut into chunks
3 onions, thinly sliced
2 garlic cloves, chopped
2 teaspoons ground cumin
1 tablespoon paprika
¹/2 teaspoon ground allspice
1–2 teaspoons chilli powder
1 tablespoon soft brown sugar
1 tablespoon red wine vinegar

1 Put the beans in a bowl, cover with water and soak overnight. Drain well. Score a cross in the base of each tomato. Put the tomatoes in a bowl of boiling water for 30 seconds, then transfer to a bowl of cold water. Drain and peel the skin away from the cross. Halve the tomatoes and remove the seeds with a teaspoon. Chop the flesh finely.

2 Heat 1 tablespoon of oil in a frying pan and add half the meat. Brown meat over medium heat for 2 minutes. Remove from the pan and repeat with the remaining meat, then remove from the pan.

3 Pour the rest of the oil into the pan and add the onion. Cook over medium heat for 5 minutes, or until translucent. Add the garlic and spices and cook, stirring, for 1 minute, or until aromatic. Add 500 ml (2 cups) water and stir. Return the meat to the pan with the beans and tomatoes. Bring to the boil, then reduce the heat to low and simmer, partially covered, for 2 hours, or until the meat is tender, stirring occasionally. Towards the end of the cooking time the mixture may start to catch, so add a little water if necessary. Stir through the sugar and vinegar, and season with salt to taste. Serve with tortillas and grated cheese.

NUTRITION PER SERVE
Protein 43 g; Fat 10 g; Carbohydrate 54 g; Dietary Fibre 10 g; Cholesterol 100 mg; 2040 kJ (486 cal)

Soak the black eye beans in a bowl of water overnight.

Drain the tomatoes then carefully peel the skin away from the cross.

Remove the seeds with a teaspoon then finely chop the flesh.

SHEPHERD'S PIE

Preparation time: 30 minutes
Total cooking time: 1 hour 20 minutes
Serves 6

1 kg (2 lb 4 oz) potatoes
30 g (1 oz) butter
2 tablespoons milk
1 tablespoon oil
1 large onion, finely chopped
1 kg (2 lb 4 oz) minced (ground)
   lamb
1 carrot, finely chopped
2 tablespoons plain (all-purpose)
   flour
250 ml (1 cup) vegetable
   stock

2 tablespoons Worcestershire
   sauce
155 g (1 cup) frozen peas

1 Peel the potatoes and cut into chunks. Cook in a large pan of boiling water for 15–20 minutes, or until tender. Drain well and return potatoes to the pan over low heat. Remove from the heat, add the butter and milk, and mash until smooth. Season with salt and pepper. Preheat the oven to 180°C (350°F/Gas 4).
2 Meanwhile, heat the oil in a large frying pan and add the onion. Cook, stirring occasionally, until soft and just beginning to colour. Add the meat, increase the heat and cook until browned.

3 Add the carrot to the pan and cook for a few minutes. Sprinkle on the flour and cook, stirring, for 1 minute. Slowly add the stock, stirring constantly. Add the Worcestershire sauce. Bring to the boil and cook for 2–3 minutes, or until the gravy thickens. Season to taste. Stir in the peas and transfer the mixture to a 2 litre (8 cup) ovenproof dish.
4 Spread the mash evenly over the meat. Use a fork to swirl the surface. Bake for 40–50 minutes, or until the potato is golden.

NUTRITION PER SERVE
Protein 40 g; Fat 20 g; Carbohydrate 30 g; Dietary Fibre 5 g; Cholesterol 105 mg; 1995 kJ (475 cal)

Cook the mince until browned, breaking up any lumps as you go.

Sprinkle the flour over the mince mixture and stir to blend it in.

Use a fork to swirl the surface of the mashed potato.

BEEF PIE

Preparation time: 35 minutes + chilling
Total cooking time: 2 hours 30 minutes
Serves 6

Filling
2 tablespoons oil
1 kg (2 lb 4 oz) trimmed chuck
　　steak, cubed
1 large onion, chopped
1 large carrot, finely chopped
2 garlic cloves, crushed
2 tablespoons plain (all-purpose)
　　flour
250 ml (1 cup) beef stock
2 teaspoons thyme leaves
1 tablespoon Worcestershire
　　sauce

Pastry
250 g (2 cups) plain
　　(all-purpose) flour
150 g (5½ oz) butter, chopped
1 egg yolk
3–4 tablespoons iced water
1 egg yolk and 1 tablespoon
　　milk, to glaze

1 Heat 1 tablespoon of the oil in a frying pan and cook the meat in batches until browned all over. Remove from the pan and set aside. Heat the remaining oil, then add the onion, carrot and garlic and cook over medium heat until browned.

2 Return the meat to the pan and stir through the flour. Cook for 1 minute, then remove from the heat and slowly stir in the stock, mixing the flour in well. Add the thyme and Worcestershire sauce, and bring to the boil. Season to taste.

3 Reduce the heat to very low, cover and simmer for 1½–2 hours, or until the meat is tender. During the last 15 minutes of cooking remove the lid and allow the liquid to reduce so that the sauce is very thick. Allow to cool completely.

4 To make the pastry, sift the flour into a bowl and add the butter. Using your fingertips, rub the butter into the flour until it resembles fine crumbs. Add the egg yolk and 2 tablespoons of iced water, and mix with a knife using a cutting action until the mixture comes together in beads, adding a little more water if necessary. Turn out onto a lightly floured surface and gather together to form a dough. Wrap in plastic wrap and refrigerate for 30 minutes.

5 Preheat the oven to 200°C (400°F/ Gas 6). Divide the pastry in two and roll out one of the pieces on a sheet of baking paper until large enough to line a 23 cm (9 inch) pie dish. Put pastry in the dish. Fill with the cold filling and roll out the remaining pastry until large enough to fully cover the dish. Dampen the edges of the pastry with your fingers dipped in water. Lay the top piece of pastry over the pie and gently press the bottom and top pieces of pastry together. Trim the overhanging edges with a sharp knife, reroll the scraps to make decorative shapes and press on the pie.

6 Cut a few slits in the top of the pastry to allow the steam to escape. Beat together the egg yolk and milk, and brush it over the top of the pie. Cook in the oven for 20–30 minutes, or until the pastry is golden and the filling is hot.

NUTRITION PER SERVE
Protein 40 g; Fat 35 g; Carbohydrate 35 g; Dietary Fibre 3 g; Cholesterol 235 mg; 2580 kJ (615 Cal)

Add the butter and rub it into the flour with your fingertips.

Mix the egg yolk and water into the flour mixture with a flat-bladed knife.

Gather the mixture together to form a smooth dough.

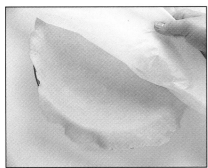

The baking paper will help you lift the pastry into the pie dish.

Spoon in the filling then top with the second piece of pastry.

Press the pieces of pastry together and trim off the excess with a sharp knife.

STEAK AND KIDNEY PUDDING

Preparation time: 25 minutes
Total cooking time: 5 hours
Serves 4

340 g (2¾ cups) self-raising
   flour
150 g (5½ oz) butter, frozen
   and grated
700 g (1 lb 9 oz) chuck steak,
   cubed
200 g (7 oz) ox kidney, cubed
1 small onion, finely chopped
2 teaspoons chopped parsley
1 tablespoon plain (all-purpose)
   flour
1 teaspoon Worcestershire sauce
185 ml (¾ cup) beef stock

1 Grease a 1.5 litre (6 cup) pudding basin with melted butter, and put a round of baking paper in the bottom. Place the empty basin in a large pan on a trivet or upturned saucer and pour in enough cold water to come halfway up the side of the basin. Remove the basin and put the water on to boil.

2 Sift the flour into a bowl and add the butter and a pinch of salt. Mix together with a flat-bladed knife and add enough water to form a soft dough. Reserve one third of the dough and roll the rest out to a circle about 1 cm (¼ inch) thick. Sprinkle with flour and fold it in half. Using a rolling pin, roll the straight edge away from you, making sure the two halves don't stick together to form a bag shape. Fit the bag into the pudding basin, leaving a little hanging over the edge. Brush out any excess flour.

3 Mix the steak, kidney, onion, parsley and flour together in a bowl. Season and add the Worcestershire sauce. Put the mixture into the pastry case and add enough stock to come three-quarters of the way up the meat. Roll out the remaining pastry to form a lid. Fold the overhanging pastry into the bowl and dampen the edge with water. Put the lid on and press the edges together.

4 Lay a sheet of foil then a sheet of baking paper on the work surface, and make a large pleat in the middle. Grease with melted butter. Place paper-side-down across the top of the basin and tie string securely around the rim and over the top of the basin to make a handle for lifting the pudding.

5 Lower the basin into the simmering water and cover with a tight-fitting lid. Cook for 5 hours, checking every hour and topping up with boiling water as needed. Serve from the basin.

NUTRITION PER SERVE
Protein 55 g; Fat 40 g; Carbohydrate 63 g; Dietary Fibre 3.7 g; Cholesterol 370 mg; 3402 kJ (813 Cal)

Roll the straight edge away from you to form a bag shape.

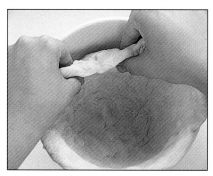

Fit the bag into the basin, leaving a little pastry hanging over the edge.

Pour in enough stock or water to come three-quarters of the way up the meat.

BEEF STROGANOFF

Preparation time: 15 minutes
Total cooking time: 15 minutes
Serves 4

500 g (1 lb 2 oz) rump steak
2 tablespoons plain (all-purpose)
   flour
2 tablespoons olive oil
1 onion, finely chopped
1 garlic clove, crushed
400 g (14 oz) button
   mushrooms, sliced

1 tablespoon tomato paste
   (purée)
300 g (10¹/₂ oz) sour cream
finely chopped parsley, to serve

1 Trim excess fat off the meat and slice it across the grain into thin pieces. Put the flour in a plastic bag and season well with salt and pepper. Add the steak and shake to coat the meat. Shake off excess flour.
2 Heat 1 tablespoon oil in a frying pan over high heat. Add the meat and cook in batches until browned. Remove from the pan and set aside.

3 Heat the remaining oil and add the onion. Cook for 2–3 minutes, or until soft and translucent, then add the garlic and stir briefly. Add the mushrooms and cook for about 3 minutes, or until soft. Stir in the tomato paste and sour cream, then add the beef strips. Stir until well combined and heated through. Sprinkle with chopped parsley and serve with rice.

NUTRITION PER SERVE
Protein 35 g; Fat 45 g; Carbohydrate 9.5 g; Dietary Fibre 3.5 g; Cholesterol 180 mg; 2365 kJ (565 Cal)

Trim any excess fat off the meat then slice into thin pieces.

Add the meat, seal the bag and shake to coat in the seasoned flour.

Cook the meat in batches until well browned all over.

CHICKEN AND BROCCOLI BAKE

Preparation time: 20 minutes
Total cooking time: 1 hour
Serves 6

30 g (1 oz) butter
4 chicken breast fillets, cubed
6 spring onions (scallions),
    sliced
2 garlic cloves, crushed
2 tablespoons plain
    (all-purpose) flour
375 ml (1½ cups) chicken stock
2 teaspoons Dijon mustard
280 g (10 oz) broccoli, cut into
    florets
1 kg (2 lb 4 oz) potatoes
2 tablespoons milk
60 g (2¼ oz) butter, extra
2 eggs
30 g (⅓ cup) flaked toasted
    almonds
chives, chopped, to garnish

1 Preheat the oven to 180°C (350°F/ Gas 4). Heat half the butter in a frying pan, and cook the chicken until browned and cooked through. Remove from the pan. In the same pan melt the remaining butter and cook the spring onion and garlic for 2 minutes. Stir in the flour. Pour in the stock and cook, stirring, until the mixture boils and thickens. Add the mustard and then stir in the chicken. Season well.

2 Meanwhile, steam the broccoli until just tender. Refresh the broccoli in iced water and drain well.

3 Boil the potatoes in salted water for 15–20 minutes, or until tender. Drain and mash well with the milk, extra butter and eggs. Put the broccoli in a

2.5 litre (10 cup) ovenproof dish and pour in the chicken mixture. Spoon the potato over the top. Sprinkle with the almonds and bake for 25 minutes, or until cooked through. Scatter the chives over the top before serving.

NUTRITION PER SERVE
Protein 25 g; Fat 20 g; Carbohydrate 25 g; Dietary Fibre 5.5 g; Cholesterol 135 mg; 1610 kJ (385 Cal)

Use a large sharp knife to cut the chicken breasts into cubes.

Add the chicken to the pan and cook in batches until browned.

Pour in the stock and stir over heat until the mixture thickens.

COQ AU VIN

Preparation time: 15 minutes
Total cooking time: 2 hours
Serves 4

1 tablespoon olive oil
12 white baby onions, peeled
3 rashers back bacon, chopped
40 g (1½ oz) butter
1.5 kg (3 lb 5 oz) chicken pieces
2 garlic cloves, crushed
375 ml (1½ cups) dry red wine
2 tablespoons brandy
1 tablespoon chopped thyme
1 bay leaf
4 parsley stalks
250 g (9 oz) button mushrooms, halved
20 g (1 oz) butter, extra
20 g (1 oz) plain (all-purpose) flour
chopped parsley, to serve

1 Preheat the oven to 170°C (325°F/ Gas 3). Heat the oil in a large frying pan and add the onions. Cook until soft, then add the bacon and cook until browned. Remove the bacon and onions and add the butter to the pan. When the butter is hot add the chicken and cook in batches until well browned. Transfer the meat to an ovenproof dish, draining it of any fat, then add the onions and bacon.

2 Tip any excess fat out of the pan and add the garlic, wine, brandy, thyme, bay leaf and parsley stalks. Bring to the boil and pour over the chicken. Cook, covered, in the oven for 1 hour 25 minutes, then add the mushrooms and cook for 30 minutes.

Drain everything through a colander and reserve the liquid. Keep the chicken warm in the oven.

3 Mix the softened butter and flour together, bring the liquid in the pan to the boil and whisk in the flour and butter paste in two batches, then reduce the heat and simmer until the liquid thickens slightly. Remove the parsley stalks and bay leaf from the chicken and return it to the ovenproof dish. Pour in the sauce, scatter on the chopped parsley and serve.

NUTRITION PER SERVE
Protein 9 g; Fat 20 g; Carbohydrate 6 g; Dietary Fibre 2.5 g; Cholesterol 53 mg; 1259 kJ (300 Cal)

Add the onions to the pan and cook until browned all over.

Cook the chicken pieces in the butter until well browned.

Whisk the flour and butter paste into the liquid in two batches.

CHICKEN CURRY

Preparation time: 25 minutes
Total cooking time: 1 hour 45 minutes
Serves 4

2 tablespoons ghee
1 kg (2 lb 4 oz) chicken
    drumsticks and thighs
1 tablespoon hot curry powder
1 tablespoon curry paste
1/2 teaspoon mustard seeds
1/2 teaspoon ground coriander
1 teaspoon paprika
1/4 teaspoon cinnamon
1/2 teaspoon cumin
1/2 teaspoon turmeric
1 tablespoon finely chopped
    coriander (cilantro) root
2 garlic cloves, crushed
2 cm (3/4 inch) piece ginger,
    grated
1 onion, chopped
1 kg (2 lb 4 oz) potatoes,
    quartered
375 ml (1 1/2 cups) chicken stock
1 tablespoon lemon juice
2 x 425 g (15 oz) cans tomatoes
250 g (9 oz) packet frozen
    spinach (silverbeet), thawed
60 ml (1/4 cup) coconut cream
shredded coriander (cilantro)
    leaves, to garnish

1 Melt 1 tablespoon of ghee in a frying pan and cook the chicken in batches for 2–3 minutes, or until browned all over. Remove. Melt the remaining ghee in the pan, add the curry powder, paste and dry spices, and cook over low heat for 1–2 minutes, or until fragrant. Increase the heat, add the coriander root, garlic, ginger and onion, and cook for 3–5 minutes, or until the onion is soft.

2 Return the chicken to the pan, add the potato and gently toss in the spices. Season generously. Pour in the stock, and stir to mix in any spices on the bottom of the pan. Add the juice and tomatoes, bring the mixture to the boil, then reduce the heat and simmer for 1–1 1/2 hours, or until the potato is tender and the meat is falling off the bones.

3 Remove the chicken from the pan, cool it slightly, then pull the meat off the bones. Return the meat to the pan. Stir in the spinach and coconut cream and cook for 3–5 minutes, or until heated through. Garnish with the coriander leaves and serve with jasmine rice.

NUTRITION PER SERVE
Protein 36 g; Fat 20 g; Carbohydrate 45 g; Dietary Fibre 12 g; Cholesterol 130 mg; 2115 kJ (505 Cal)

Melt the ghee, then cook the chicken in batches until browned all over.

Cook the curry powder, curry paste and dry spices until fragrant.

Gently toss the chicken and potatoes in the spices to coat.

CHICKEN AND MUSHROOM CASSEROLE

Preparation time: 20 minutes
Total cooking time: 1 hour
Serves 4

20 g (1 oz) dried porcini mushrooms
30 g (1/4 cup) plain (all-purpose) flour
1.5 kg (3 lb 5 oz) chicken pieces
2 tablespoons oil
1 large onion, chopped
2 garlic cloves, crushed
60 ml (1/4 cup) chicken stock
80 ml (1/3 cup) white wine

425 g (15 oz) can tomatoes
1 tablespoon balsamic vinegar
3 thyme sprigs
1 bay leaf
300 g (10 1/2 oz) field mushrooms, thickly sliced

1 Preheat the oven to 180°C (350°F/ Gas 4). Put the porcini mushrooms in a bowl and cover with 60 ml (1/4 cup) boiling water. Leave to rehydrate for 5 minutes.

2 Season the flour with salt and pepper. Lightly toss the chicken in flour to coat. Shake off any excess.

3 Heat the oil in a casserole, and cook the chicken in batches until well browned. Set aside. Add the onion and garlic to the casserole and cook until the onion softens. Stir in the chicken stock.

4 Put the chicken in the casserole with the porcini mushrooms (and any remaining liquid), wine, tomatoes, vinegar, thyme and bay leaf. Cover and cook in the oven for 30 minutes.

5 After 30 minutes, add the field mushrooms. Return to the oven and cook, uncovered, for a further 15–20 minutes, or until the sauce thickens slightly. Serve immediately.

NUTRITION PER SERVE
Protein 55 g; Fat 10 g; Carbohydrate 7 g; Dietary Fibre 4 g; Cholesterol 115 mg; 1515 kJ (360 Cal)

Cover the porcini mushrooms with boiling water and soak until rehydrated.

Lightly toss the chicken pieces in the flour and shake off any excess.

Add the chicken to the casserole and cook in batches until browned.

CHICKEN CACCIATORE

Preparation time: 45 minutes
Total cooking time: 1 hour 20 minutes
Serves 4

4 medium tomatoes
1.5 kg (3 lb 5 oz) chicken pieces
20 g (1 oz) butter
1 tablespoon oil
20 g (1 oz) butter, extra
1 large onion, chopped
2 garlic cloves, chopped
1 small green capsicum
    (pepper), chopped
150 g (5½ oz) mushrooms,
    sliced thickly
1 tablespoon plain (all-purpose)
    flour
250 ml (1 cup) white wine
1 tablespoon white wine
    vinegar
2 tablespoons tomato paste
    (purée)
90 g (½ cup) small black olives
20 g (⅓ cup) chopped parsley

1 Score a cross in the base of each tomato. Put the tomatoes in a bowl of boiling water for 30 seconds, then transfer to a bowl of cold water. Drain and peel the skin away from the cross. Halve the tomatoes and remove the seeds with a teaspoon and chop the flesh. Preheat the oven to 180°C (350°F/Gas 4).
2 Remove excess fat from the chicken pieces and pat dry with paper towels. Heat half the butter and oil in a large flameproof casserole. Cook half the chicken over high heat until browned all over, then set aside. Heat the remaining butter and oil and cook the remaining chicken. Set aside.
3 Heat the extra butter in the casserole and cook the onion and garlic for 2–3 minutes. Add the capsicum and mushrooms, and cook, stirring, for 3 minutes. Stir in the flour and cook for 1 minute. Add the wine, vinegar, tomato and tomato paste and cook, stirring, for 2 minutes, or until slightly thickened.
4 Return the chicken to the casserole and make sure it is covered by the tomato and onion mixture. Place in the oven and cook, covered, for 1 hour, or until the chicken is tender. Stir in the olives and parsley. Season and serve with pasta.

NUTRITION PER SERVE
Protein 55 g; Fat 15 g; Carbohydrate 9.5 g; Dietary Fibre 5 g; Cholesterol 125 mg; 1675 kJ (401 Cal)

Drain the tomatoes then peel away the skin from the cross.

Cut the tomatoes in half and remove the seeds with a teaspoon.

Cook the chicken in batches over high heat until browned all over.

APRICOT CHICKEN

Preparation time: 10 minutes
Total cooking time: 1 hour
Serves 6

6 chicken thigh cutlets, skin
    removed
425 ml (15 fl oz) tin apricot
    nectar
40 g (1½ oz) packet French
    onion soup mix
425 g (15 fl oz) can apricot
    halves in juice, drained
60 g (¼ cup) sour cream

1 Preheat the oven to 180°C (350°F/Gas 4). Put the chicken thigh cutlets in an ovenproof dish. Mix the apricot nectar with the French onion soup mix until well combined and pour liquid over the chicken pieces.
2 Bake, covered, for 50 minutes, then add the apricot halves and bake for a further 5 minutes. Stir in the sour cream just before serving. This is delicious served with creamy mashed potato or boiled rice to soak up the juices.

NUTRITION PER SERVE
Protein 23 g; Fat 6 g; Carbohydrate 10 g; Dietary Fibre 0 g; Cholesterol 63 mg; 780 kJ (187 Cal)

Pour in the apricot nectar and stir to combine with the soup mix.

Add the apricot halves to the chicken and bake for 5 minutes more.

*Chicken Cacciatore (top)
and Apricot Chicken*

SPINACH AND RICOTTA CANNELLONI

Preparation time: 45 minutes
Total cooking time: 1 hour
Serves 4

Filling
20 g (1 oz) butter
1 small onion, finely chopped
2 garlic cloves, crushed
3 bunches English spinach,
   trimmed and finely shredded
300 g (10$^{1}/_{2}$ oz) ricotta cheese
1 tablespoon oregano

Sauce
1 tablespoon olive oil
1 small onion, finely chopped
2 garlic cloves, crushed
440 g (1 lb) can tomatoes
125 ml ($^{1}/_{2}$ cup) tomato pasta
   sauce
1 teaspoon dried oregano
2 teaspoons Dijon mustard
1 tablespoon balsamic vinegar
1 teaspoon sugar

375 g (13 oz) fresh lasagne
   sheets
75 g ($^{1}/_{2}$ cup) grated mozzarella
   cheese
50 g ($^{1}/_{2}$ cup) grated Parmesan
   cheese

1 Preheat the oven to 180°C (350°F/ Gas 4). Cut the pasta sheets into twelve 12 cm (5 inch) squares. Bring a pan of salted water to the boil, blanch the lasagne in batches for 1–2 minutes, then drain flat on a damp tea towel.
2 Melt the butter in a pan and add the onion and garlic. Cook for 3–5 minutes until onion is soft. Add the spinach and cook for 5 minutes, or until wilted and moisture has evaporated. Remove from the heat. When cool, combine with the ricotta and oregano in a food processor. Process until smooth and season.
3 To make the sauce, heat the oil in a pan, cook the onion and garlic over low heat for 8–10 minutes. Add the rest of the sauce ingredients. Bring to the boil, reduce the heat and simmer for 10–15 minutes, or until sauce thickens.
4 Lightly grease a 2 litre (8 cup) ovenproof dish. Spread one third of the sauce over the base, and spoon 1$^{1}/_{2}$ tablespoons of spinach onto one side of each lasagne square, leaving a thin border. Roll up the pasta to cover the filling and place in the dish seam side down. Repeat with all the sheets, spacing the cannelloni evenly in the dish. Spoon in the remaining sauce and sprinkle with the cheeses. Bake for 30–35 minutes, or until the cheese is golden. Stand for 5 minutes before serving.

NUTRITION PER SERVE
Protein 25 g; Fat 27 g; Carbohydrate 35 g; Dietary Fibre 5 g; Cholesterol 70 mg; 1970 kJ (470 Cal)

Blanch the lasagne in salted boiling water in batches.

Lay the lasagne squares out flat on a clean damp tea towel to drain.

Spoon the spinach mixture onto one side of the pasta square and roll up.

VEGETABLE CURRY

Preparation time: 20 minutes
Total cooking time: 35 minutes
Serves 4

2 tablespoons oil
2 onions, finely chopped
2 garlic cloves, crushed
2 teaspoons grated ginger
1–2 teaspoons chilli powder
1 tablespoon ground cumin
1 tablespoon ground
    coriander
1 teaspoon turmeric
2 teaspoons mustard seeds
2 carrots, sliced

150 g (5¹/2 oz) green beans,
    chopped
400 g (14 oz) can crushed
    tomatoes
125 ml (¹/2 cup) vegetable stock
2 slender eggplants (aubergines)
2 zucchini (courgettes)
500 g (1 lb 2 oz) pumpkin,
    peeled
400 g (14 oz) can chickpeas,
    rinsed and drained

1 Heat the oil in a large frying pan. Cook the onion over low heat for 5 minutes, or until soft. Add the garlic, ginger and spices, and cook for 1 minute, stirring, until fragrant.
2 Add the carrot, beans, tomato and stock to the pan and stir thoroughly. Bring to the boil, and simmer for 5 minutes.
3 Meanwhile, thickly slice the eggplants and zucchini. Cut the pumpkin into cubes. Add all the vegetables to the pan. Simmer, over low heat with the pan partially covered, for 30 minutes, or until the vegetables are tender, but still hold their shape. Add the chickpeas and cook for 10 minutes, or until heated through. Season and serve with rice.

NUTRITION PER SERVE
Protein 13 g; Fat 8 g; Carbohydrate 30 g; Dietary Fibre 13 g; Cholesterol 0 mg; 1075 kJ (255 Cal)

Add the garlic, ginger and spices and stir until fragrant.

Stir the carrot, beans, tomato and stock in with the spice mixture.

Thickly slice the eggplant and zucchini and cut the pumpkin into cubes.

VEGETABLE TAGINE

Preparation time: 20 minutes
Total cooking time: 40 minutes
Serves 4

1 large potato
1 large carrot
1 turnip or swede (rutabaga),
    peeled
150 g (5¹/2 oz) sweet potato
400 g (14 oz) can tomatoes
375 ml (1¹/2 cups) chicken
    or vegetable stock
2 tablespoons olive oil
2 red onions, chopped
8 garlic cloves, chopped
1 large red chilli, seeded
    and chopped
1 tablespoon ground cumin
1 cinnamon stick
1 zucchini
2 baby eggplants (aubergines)
100 g (3¹/2 oz) blanched
    almonds
125 g (4¹/2 oz) dried apricots

1 Cut the potato, carrot, turnip or swede and sweet potato into chunks. Place them in a large saucepan and add the tomatoes and enough of the stock to cover. Bring slowly to the boil then cover and simmer for 15 minutes, or until the vegetables are just tender.
2 Meanwhile, heat the oil in a frying pan. Cook, stirring, the onion, garlic and chilli for 5 minutes, or until tender. Add the cumin and cinnamon stick and cook over low heat for 3 minutes.
3 Add the onion mixture to the pan with the vegetables. Cut the zucchini and eggplants into large pieces and add to the vegetables with the almonds and apricots. Stir to combine and bring slowly to the boil. Reduce the heat and simmer, covered, for 10 minutes. If still liquid, simmer, uncovered, for a further 5 minutes—the vegetables should be tender and the liquid thickened. Season to taste with salt and ground black pepper. Serve with harissa and couscous.

NUTRITION PER SERVE
Protein 10 g; Fat 25 g; Carbohydrate 35 g;
Dietary Fibre 12 g; Cholesterol 0 mg;
1670 kJ (399 Cal)

Wearing protective gloves, remove the seeds and chop the chilli.

Use a sharp knife to cut the vegetables into large pieces.

Heat the oil in a frying pan and cook the onion, garlic and chilli.

Cut the zucchini and eggplants into large pieces and add them to the pan.

OSSO BUCCO WITH GREMOLATA

Preparation time: 30 minutes
Total cooking time: 2 hours 40 minutes
Serves 4

2 tablespoons olive oil
1 onion, finely chopped
1 garlic clove, crushed
1 kg (2 lb 4 oz) veal shin slices
2 tablespoons plain
    (all-purpose) flour
410 g (14 oz) can chopped
    tomatoes
250 ml (1 cup) white wine

250 ml (1 cup) chicken stock

Gremolata
2 tablespoons chopped parsley
2 teaspoons grated lemon zest
1 teaspoon finely chopped garlic

1 Heat 1 tablespoon oil in a large shallow casserole. Add the onion and cook over low heat until soft. Add the garlic. Cook for 1 minute, then remove from the dish.
2 Heat the remaining oil and brown the veal in batches, then remove. Return the onion to the casserole and stir in the flour. Cook for 30 seconds and remove from the heat. Stir in the tomatoes, wine and stock, mixing well with the flour. Return the veal to the casserole.
3 Return to the heat and bring to the boil, stirring. Cover and reduce the heat to low so that the casserole is just simmering. Cook for $2^{1/2}$ hours, or until the meat is very tender and falling off the bones.
4 To make the gremolata, combine the parsley, zest and garlic in a bowl. Sprinkle the gremolata over the the osso bucco and serve with rice.

NUTRITION PER SERVE
Protein 50 g; Fat 15 g; Carbohydrate 9.5 g; Dietary Fibre 2.5 g; Cholesterol 165 mg; 1700 kJ (405 Cal)

Heat the oil and cook the veal pieces in batches until browned.

Add the tomatoes, white wine and stock, and mix until well combined.

Make the gremolata by mixing together the parsley, lemon zest and garlic.

VEAL GOULASH

Preparation time: 25 minutes
Total cooking time: 2 hours
Serves 4

500 g (1 lb 2 oz) veal, cut into
    2.5 cm (1 inch) pieces
2 tablespoons plain (all-purpose)
    flour
2 tablespoons olive oil
2 onions, thinly sliced
2 garlic cloves, finely chopped
1 tablespoon sweet Hungarian
    paprika
1 teaspoon ground cumin
440 g (1 lb) can chopped
    tomatoes

2 carrots, sliced
1/2 red capsicum (pepper),
    chopped
1/2 green capsicum, (pepper)
    chopped
250 ml (1 cup) beef stock
125 ml (1/2 cup) red wine
125 ml (1/2 cup) sour cream
chopped parsley, to garnish

1 Put the veal and flour in a plastic bag and shake to coat the veal with flour. Shake off any excess. Heat 1 tablespoon oil in a large deep saucepan over medium heat. Brown the meat well in batches, then remove the meat and set aside.
2 Add the remaining oil to the pan. Cook the onion, garlic, paprika and cumin for 5 minutes, stirring frequently. Return the meat and any juices to the pan with the tomato, carrot and capsicum. Cover and cook for 10 minutes.
3 Add the stock and wine and season with salt and pepper. Stir well, then cover and simmer over very low heat for 1 1/2 hours. Stir in half the sour cream, season with more salt and pepper if needed and serve garnished with parsley and the remaining sour cream. Delicious served with buttered boiled small potatoes or noodles.

NUTRITION PER SERVE
Protein 30 g; Fat 25 g; Carbohydrate 15 g; Dietary Fibre 4.5 g; Cholesterol 144 mg; 1790 kJ (430 Cal)

Remove any excess fat then cut the veal into 2.5 cm (1 inch) pieces.

Put the veal and flour in a plastic bag and shake to coat.

Heat the oil in a pan, add the veal and brown well in batches.

SLOW-COOKED SHANKS

Preparation time: 20 minutes
Total cooking time: 3 hours
Serves 4

2 tablespoons oil
4 lamb shanks
2 red onions, sliced
10 garlic cloves, peeled
400 g (14 oz) can chopped
    tomatoes

125 ml (¹/2 cup) dry white wine
1 bay leaf
1 teaspoon grated lemon zest
1 large red capsicum (pepper),
    chopped
3 tablespoons chopped parsley

1 Preheat the oven to 170°C (325°F/ Gas 3). Heat the oil in a large casserole, add the shanks in batches and cook over high heat until browned all over.
2 Add the onion and garlic, and cook until softened, then add the tomato, wine, bay leaf, lemon zest, capsicum and 125 ml (¹/2 cup) water and bring to the boil. Cover and cook in the oven for 2–2¹/2 hours, or until the meat is tender and the sauce is thickened. Season to taste.
3 Sprinkle the parsley over the top and serve with couscous.

NUTRITION PER SERVE
Protein 35 g; Fat 10 g; Carbohydrate 9 g; Dietary Fibre 4.5 g; Cholesterol 85 mg; 1275 kJ (305 Cal)

Heat the oil in a pan and brown the shanks in batches.

Add the onion and garlic to the pan and cook until softened

Add the tomato, wine, bay leaf, lemon zest, capsicum and water.

LAMB CASSEROLE WITH BEANS

Preparation time: 25 minutes +
   overnight soaking
Total cooking time: 2 hours 15 minutes
Serves 6

300 g (1½ cups) borlotti beans
1 kg (2 lb 4 oz) boned leg lamb
1½ tablespoons olive oil
2 rashers back bacon, chopped
1 large onion, chopped
2 garlic cloves, crushed
1 large carrot, chopped
500 ml (2 cups) dry red wine
1 tablespoon tomato paste
   (purée)

375 ml (1½ cups) beef stock
2 rosemary sprigs
2 thyme sprigs

1 Put the beans in a bowl and cover with plenty of water. Leave to soak overnight, then drain well.
2 Preheat the oven to 160°C (315°F/ Gas 2–3). Trim any excess fat from the lamb and cut into 3 cm (1¼ inch) pieces.
3 Heat 1 tablespoon oil in a large casserole. Add half the meat and toss over medium heat for 2 minutes, or until browned. Remove from the pan and repeat with remaining lamb. Remove from the pan.
4 Heat the remaining oil in the casserole and add the bacon and onion.

Cook over medium heat for 3 minutes, or until the onion is soft. Add the garlic and carrot, and cook for 1 minute, or until aromatic.
5 Return the meat and any juices to the pan, increase the heat to high and add the wine. Bring to the boil and cook for 2 minutes. Add the beans, tomato paste, stock, rosemary and thyme, bring to the boil, then cover and cook in the oven for 2 hours, or until the meat is tender. Stir occasionally during cooking. Skim off any excess fat, remove the herb sprigs and season. Serve with bread.

NUTRITION PER SERVE
Protein 50 g; Fat 10 g; Carbohydrate 48 g; Dietary Fibre 9 g; Cholesterol 117 mg; 2367 kJ (565 Cal)

Remove any excess fat from the lamb then cut it into pieces.

Heat the oil then add the lamb and toss until browned all over.

Return the meat and juices to the pan, add the wine, and bring to the boil.

LANCASHIRE HOTPOT

Preparation time: 20 minutes
Total cooking time: 2 hours
Serves 8

8 lamb forequarter chops
4 lamb kidneys
30 g (1/4 cup) plain (all-purpose)
    flour
50 g (1³/4 oz) butter
4 potatoes, thinly sliced
2 large onions, sliced
1 large carrot, chopped
440 ml (1³/4 cups) beef stock
2 teaspoons chopped thyme
1 bay leaf
melted butter, extra

1 Preheat the oven to 160°C (315°F/ Gas 2–3), and brush a large casserole dish with melted butter or oil. Trim the chops of excess fat and sinew, then remove the cores from the kidneys and cut into quarters. Toss the chops and kidneys in flour, shaking off and reserving the excess. Heat the butter in a frying pan and brown the chops quickly on both sides. Remove the chops from the pan and brown the kidneys.
2 Layer half the potato slices in the base of the casserole and top with the chops and kidneys.
3 Add the onion and carrot to the pan and cook until the carrot begins to brown. Layer on top of the chops and kidneys. Sprinkle the reserved flour over the base of the pan and fry, stirring, until dark brown. Gradually pour in the stock and bring to the boil, stirring. Season well and add the thyme and bay leaf. Reduce the heat and simmer for 10 minutes. Pour into the casserole.
4 Layer the remaining potato over the meat and vegetables. Cover and cook in the oven for 1¹/4 hours. Increase the temperature to 180°C (350°F/Gas 4), brush the potato with the extra butter and cook, uncovered, for 20 minutes, or until the potato is brown.

NUTRITION PER SERVE
Protein 38 g; Fat 11 g; Carbohydrate 13 g; Dietary Fibre 2 g; Cholesterol 175 mg; 1285 kJ (305 Cal)

Remove the cores from the kidneys and cut them into quarters.

Cover the base with potato slices then add the chops and kidneys.

Layer the remaining potato slices over the meat and vegetables.

ITALIAN SAUSAGE CASSEROLE

Preparation time: 15 minutes
Total cooking time: 45 minutes
Serves 4

2 large red capsicums (peppers)
1 tablespoon olive oil
2 large red onions, sliced into
    thick wedges
2 garlic cloves, finely chopped
600 g (1 lb 5 oz) Italian-style
    thin pork sausages
300 g (10½ oz) can chickpeas,
    drained
150 g (5½ oz) flat mushrooms,
    thickly sliced
125 ml (½ cup) dry white wine
2 bay leaves

2 teaspoons chopped rosemary
400 g (14 oz) can chopped
    tomatoes

1 Cut the capsicums into large pieces, removing the seeds and membrane. Place skin-side up, under a hot grill (broiler) until the skin blackens and blisters. Allow to cool in a plastic bag. Peel away the skin, and slice diagonally into thick strips.
2 Meanwhile, heat the oil in a large non-stick frying pan. Add the onion and garlic, and stir over medium heat for 6 minutes, or until the onion is soft and browned. Remove the onion from the pan and set aside. Add the sausages to the same pan. Cook over medium heat, turning occasionally, for 8 minutes, or until the sausages are browned. Remove the sausages and

slice diagonally into 3 cm (1¼ inch) pieces.
3 Combine the capsicum, onion, sausage, chickpeas and mushrooms in the pan and cook over high heat.
4 Add the wine, bay leaves and rosemary. Bring to the boil, then reduce the heat to low and simmer for 3 minutes. Stir in the tomatoes and simmer for 20 minutes, or until the sauce has thickened slightly. Remove the bay leaves and season to taste with sugar, salt and pepper. Serve with fettucine, grilled ciabatta bread, mashed potato, polenta, or Parmesan shavings.

NUTRITION PER SERVE
Protein 20 g; Fat 25 g; Carbohydrate 25 g; Dietary Fibre 9.5 g; Cholesterol 50 mg; 1695 kJ (405 Cal)

Grill the capsicums under a hot grill until the skin blackens and blisters.

Remove the skin from the cooled capsicums and slice them into thin strips.

Use a pair of tongs to hold the sausages as you slice them into pieces.

ROAST CHICKEN WITH BREADCRUMB STUFFING

Preparation time: 40 minutes
Total cooking time: 1 hour 30 minutes
Serves 6

3 rashers back bacon, chopped
6 slices wholegrain bread,
    crusts removed
3 spring onions (scallions),
    chopped
2 tablespoons chopped pecans
2 teaspoons currants
15 g (1/4 cup) chopped parsley
1 egg, lightly beaten
60 ml (1/4 cup) milk
1.4 kg (3 lb 4 oz) chicken
40 g (1 1/2 oz) butter, melted
1 tablespoon oil
1 tablespoon soy sauce
1 garlic clove, crushed
375 ml (1 1/2 cups) chicken stock
1 tablespoon plain (all-purpose)
    flour

1 Preheat the oven to 180°C (350°F/ Gas 4). Cook the bacon in a dry frying pan over high heat for 5 minutes, or until crisp. Cut the bread into small cubes and place in a bowl. Mix in the bacon, spring onion, pecans, currants, parsley and combined egg and milk. Season with salt and pepper.

2 Remove the giblets and any large amounts of fat from the cavity of the chicken. Pat the chicken dry with paper towels. Spoon the bacon mixture into the chicken cavity. Tuck the wings under the chicken and tie the legs securely with string.

3 Place the chicken on a rack in a deep baking dish. Brush with the combined butter, oil and soy sauce. Pour any remaining mixture into the baking dish with the garlic and half the stock. Roast the chicken for 1–1 1/4 hours, or until brown and tender, basting occasionally with the pan juices. Pierce between the thigh and body to the bone and check that any juices running out are clear. Put the chicken on a serving dish. Cover loosely with foil and leave in a warm place for 5 minutes before carving.

4 Discard all but 1 tablespoon of the pan juices from the baking dish. Transfer the baking dish to the stove. Add the flour to the pan juices and

blend to a smooth paste. Stir constantly over low heat for 5 minutes, or until the mixture browns. Gradually add the remaining stock and stir until the mixture boils and thickens. (Add a little extra stock or water if the gravy is too thick.) Season the gravy with salt and pepper and strain into a jug. Serve the chicken with snowpeas (mangetouts) and roast potatoes.

NUTRITION PER SERVE
Protein 33 g; Fat 20 g; Carbohydrate 15 g;
Dietary Fibre 3 g; Cholesterol 110 mg;
1530 kJ (365 Cal)

Pat the chicken dry and spoon the stuffing into the chicken cavity.

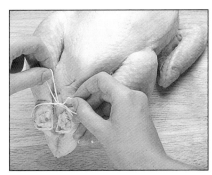

Tuck the wings under the chicken and tie the legs securely with string.

TRADITIONAL ROAST BEEF WITH YORKSHIRE PUDDINGS

Preparation time: 15 minutes
Total cooking time: 1 hour 45 minutes
Serves 6

2.5 kg (5 lb 8 oz) piece roasting
   beef
2 garlic cloves, crushed
1 tablespoon plain (all-purpose)
   flour
2 tablespoons red wine
315 ml (1¼ cups) beef stock

Yorkshire puddings
2 cups (250 g) plain
   (all-purpose) flour
4 eggs
400 ml (14 fl oz) milk

1 Preheat the oven to 240°C (475°F/ Gas 9). Rub the beef with garlic and pepper. Put on a rack in a baking dish, and bake for 15 minutes.
2 To make the puddings, sift the flour and a pinch of salt into a bowl, and make a well in the centre. Add the eggs and whisk. Gradually pour in the milk and whisk to a smooth batter. Pour into a jug, cover and leave for 30 minutes.
3 Reduce the heat to 180°C (350°F/ Gas 4), and roast the meat for 50–60 minutes for a rare result, or a little longer for well done. Cover the meat loosely with foil and leave in a warm place for 10–15 minutes. Increase the oven temperature to 220°C (425°F/ Gas 7).
4 Pour the pan juices into a jug, then separate the oil from the meat juices, reserving both. Put 1 teaspoon of the oil in each hole of a 12-hole, deep patty

pan. Heat in the oven for 2–3 minutes, or until just smoking. Pour in the batter to three-quarters full, put in the oven and bake for 5 minutes. Reduce the oven to 200°C (400°F/Gas 6) and bake for 10 minutes, or until risen and golden.
5 Meanwhile, put the baking dish with the reserved meat juices on the stove over low heat. Add the flour and stir, scraping the bottom of the pan to release any sediment. Cook over medium heat, stirring constantly,

until the flour is browned. Combine the wine and stock, and gradually stir into the flour mixture. Cook, stirring constantly, until the gravy boils and thickens. Simmer for 3 minutes.
6 Slice the beef and serve with the gravy, Yorkshire puddings, Brussels sprouts and roast potatoes.

NUTRITION PER SERVE
Protein 100 g; Fat 20 g; Carbohydrate 35 g; Dietary Fibre 2 g; Cholesterol 335 mg; 3085 kJ (740 Cal)

Rub garlic over the outside of the meat and season with ground pepper.

Pour the pan juices into a jug and allow the oil to separate from the meat juices.

Pour the pudding batter into the holes until three-quarters full.

ROAST LEG OF PORK

Preparation time: 30 minutes
Total cooking time: 3 hours 45 minutes
Serves 8

4 kg (9 lb) leg of pork
oil and salt, to rub on pork

Gravy
1 tablespoon brandy or Calvados
2 tablespoons plain (all-purpose)
    flour
375 ml (1½ cups) chicken stock
125 ml (½ cup) unsweetened
    apple juice

1 Preheat the oven to 250°C (500°F/ Gas 10). Score the rind of the pork with a sharp knife at 3 cm (1 inch) intervals. Rub in some oil and salt to ensure crisp crackling. Place the pork, rind-side-up, on a rack in a large baking dish.

2 Add a little water to the dish. Roast for 30 minutes, or until the rind begins to crackle and bubble. Reduce the heat to 180°C (350°F/Gas 4). Roast for 2 hours 40 minutes, then roast for a further 30 minutes. The pork is cooked if the juices run clear when the flesh is pierced with a skewer. Do not cover the pork or the crackling will soften. Leave in a warm place for 10 minutes.

3 To make the gravy, drain off all except 2 tablespoons of the pan juices from the baking dish. Place on top of the stove over medium heat, add the brandy and stir to lift the sediment from the bottom of the pan. Cook for 1 minute. Remove from the heat, stir in the flour and mix well. Return the pan to the heat and cook for 2 minutes, stirring constantly. Gradually add the stock and apple juice, and cook, stirring, until the gravy boils and thickens. Season to taste. Slice the pork and serve with the crackling, gravy, apple sauce, baked apple wedges and vegetables.

NUTRITION PER SERVE
Protein 157 g; Fat 8.5 g; Carbohydrate 2.4 g; Dietary Fibre 0 g; Cholesterol 305 mg; 3050 kJ (730 Cal)

Use a sharp knife to score the pork zest at regular intervals.

Rub oil and salt into the zest to make sure the crackling will be crisp.

Test the pork by piercing with a skewer— if the juices run clear, the flesh is cooked.

45

NOT-SO-LIGHT SUPPERS

ROAST PUMPKIN SOUP

Preparation time: 20 minutes
Total cooking time: 55 minutes
Serves 6

1.25 kg (2 lb 12 oz) butternut
   pumpkin (squash), peeled
   and cut into chunks
2 tablespoons olive oil
1 large onion, chopped
2 teaspoons ground cumin
1 large carrot, chopped
1 celery stalk, chopped
1 litre (4 cups) chicken or
   vegetable stock
sour cream, to serve
finely chopped parsley, to serve
ground nutmeg, to serve

1 Preheat the oven to 180°C (350°F/ Gas 4). Put the pumpkin on a greased baking tray and lightly brush with half the olive oil. Bake for 25 minutes, or until softened and slightly browned around the edges.

2 Heat the remaining oil in a large pan. Cook the onion and cumin for 2 minutes, then add the carrot and celery and cook for 3 minutes more, stirring frequently. Add the roasted pumpkin and stock. Bring to the boil, then reduce the heat and simmer for 20 minutes.

3 Allow to cool a little, then purée in batches in a blender or food processor. Return the soup to the pan and gently reheat without boiling. Season to taste with salt and ground black pepper. Top with sour cream and sprinkle with chopped parsley and ground nutmeg before serving.

NUTRITION PER SERVE
Protein 5 g; Fat 8.5 g; Carbohydrate 15 g; Dietary Fibre 3.5 g; Cholesterol 4.5 mg; 665 kJ (160 Cal)

COOK'S FILE

Note: Butternut pumpkin has a sweeter flavour than other varieties.

Lightly brush the pumpkin chunks with oil and bake until softened.

Put the cooled mixture in a blender or food processor and purée in batches.

FRENCH ONION SOUP

Preparation time: 30 minutes
Total cooking time: 1 hour 30 minutes
Serves 4

50 g (1³/₄ oz) butter
1 tablespoon olive oil
1 kg (2 lb 4 oz) onions, thinly
    sliced into rings
3 x 420 g (15 oz) cans chicken
    or beef consommé
125 ml (¹/₂ cup) dry sherry
¹/₂ baguette
35 g (¹/₃ cup) grated Parmesan
    cheese
125 g (1 cup) finely grated
    Cheddar or Gruyère cheese
1 tablespoon finely chopped
    fresh parsley, to serve

1 Heat the butter and oil in a large saucepan, then add the onion and cook, stirring frequently, over low heat for 45 minutes, or until softened and translucent. Be careful not to rush this stage—cook the onion thoroughly so that it caramelizes for full flavour.

2 Add the consommé, sherry and 250 ml (1 cup) water. Bring to the boil, then reduce the heat and simmer for 30 minutes. Season.

3 Meanwhile, cut four thick slices of bread and put in a single layer under a hot grill (broiler). Toast one side, turn and sprinkle with Parmesan, and toast until crisp and golden and the cheese has melted.

4 Put the toast into serving bowls. Ladle in the hot soup, sprinkle with the Cheddar and parsley and serve.

NUTRITION PER SERVE
Protein 20 g; Fat 30 g; Carbohydrate 30 g; Dietary Fibre 5 g; Cholesterol 70 mg; 1925 kJ (460 Cal)

Using a large sharp knife, cut the onions into thin rings.

Heat the oil and butter in a large pan and add the onion.

Stir frequently over low heat until the onion is softened and translucent.

CHICKEN AND CORN SOUP

Preparation time: 15 minutes
Total cooking time: 20 minutes
Serves 6

3 corn cobs
1 tablespoon vegetable oil
4 spring onions (scallions), finely chopped
2 teaspoons grated ginger
1 litre (4 cups) chicken stock
1 tablespoon rice wine, mirin or sherry
1 tablespoon light soy sauce

½ small barbecued chicken, shredded
1 tablespoon cornflour (cornstarch)
1 teaspoon sesame oil
420 g (15 oz) can creamed corn
thyme sprigs, to garnish

1 Cut the corn kernels from the cobs —you will need about 400 g (2 cups). Heat the oil in a large pan, and add the spring onion and ginger. Cook for 1 minute, or until softened, then add the corn, stock, rice wine and soy sauce. Bring slowly to the boil, then reduce the heat and simmer for 10 minutes, or until the kernels are cooked through. Add the chicken.

2 In a bowl, blend the cornflour with 3 tablespoons water or stock to make a smooth paste. Add to the soup with the sesame oil and simmer, stirring continuously, until slightly thickened. Stir in the creamed corn and heat for 2–3 minutes without allowing to boil. Season with salt and ground black pepper and serve hot, garnished with thyme sprigs.

NUTRITION PER SERVE
Protein 14 g; Fat 8 g; Carbohydrate 30 g; Dietary Fibre 5 g; Cholesterol 45 mg; 1077 kJ (255 Cal)

Use a fork to shred the meat from the barbecued chicken.

Remove the husk from the corn cobs and cut off the kernels.

Blend the cornflour and water or stock to form a smooth paste.

OXTAIL SOUP

Preparation time: 20 minutes + chilling
Total cooking time: 3 hours 20 minutes
Serves 4

2 tablespoons plain (all-purpose)
   flour
1 kg (2 lb 4 oz) oxtail, chopped
   into 5 cm (2 inch) pieces
1 tablespoon oil
2 litres (8 cups) beef stock
1 onion, chopped
1 celery stalk, chopped
2 carrots, chopped
1 turnip, peeled and chopped
3 whole cloves
12 peppercorns

2 bay leaves
2 tablespoons port
1 tablespoon tomato paste
   (purée)
20 g (¹/₃ cup) chopped parsley

1 Season 1 tablespoon of the flour and put it in a plastic bag with the oxtail and shake to coat. Shake off excess flour. Heat the oil in a saucepan, add the oxtail and cook in batches, tossing continually, for 5 minutes, or until evenly browned. Return all the oxtail to the pan.

2 Add the stock, vegetables, cloves, peppercorns, bay leaves, ¹/₂ teaspoon salt and 375 ml (1¹/₂ cups) water. Bring slowly to the boil then reduce the heat and simmer, covered, for 3 hours.

3 Strain the vegetables and meat, reserving the liquid. Discard the vegetables and leave the meat to cool. Pull the meat from the bone, shred and refrigerate. Meanwhile, refrigerate the stock until the fat has solidified on the surface. Spoon the fat off and add the meat.

4 Put the soup in a clean pan. Mix together the remaining flour, port and tomato paste, and add to the pan. Bring to the boil, stirring, until the soup thickens. Simmer for 10 minutes, then stir in the parsley.

NUTRITION PER SERVE
Protein 25 g; Fat 7.5 g; Carbohydrate 9.5 g; Dietary Fibre 2.5 g; Cholesterol 65 mg; 1700 kJ (405 Cal)

Put the seasoned flour and oxtail pieces in a plastic bag and shake to coat.

Heat the oil and cook the oxtail pieces in batches until browned.

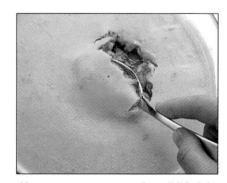

Use a spoon to remove the solidified fat from the surface of the stock.

ASIAN CHICKEN NOODLE SOUP

Preparation time: 20 minutes +
10 minutes soaking
Total cooking time: 10 minutes
Serves 4

3 dried Chinese
    mushrooms
185 g (6½ oz) thin dry egg
    noodles
1 tablespoon oil
4 spring onions (scallions),
    julienned
1 tablespoon soy sauce
2 tablespoons rice wine, mirin
    or sherry

1.25 litres (5 cups) chicken
    stock
½ small barbecued chicken,
    shredded
50 g (1¾ oz) sliced ham,
    cut into strips
90 g (1 cup) bean sprouts
fresh coriander (cilantro) leaves
    and thinly sliced red chilli,
    to garnish

1 Soak the mushrooms in boiling water for 10 minutes to soften them. Squeeze dry then remove the tough stems and slice the mushrooms thinly.
2 Cook the noodles in a large saucepan of boiling water for 3 minutes, or according to the manufacturer's directions. Drain and cut the noodles into shorter lengths with scissors.

3 Heat the oil in a large saucepan. Add the mushrooms and spring onion. Cook for 1 minute, then add the soy sauce, rice wine and stock. Bring slowly to the boil and cook for 1 minute. Reduce the heat then add the noodles, chicken, ham and bean sprouts. Heat through for 2 minutes without allowing to boil.
4 Use tongs to divide the noodles among four serving bowls, ladle in the remaining mixture, and garnish with the coriander leaves and sliced chilli.

NUTRITION PER SERVE
Protein 25 g; Fat 10 g; Carbohydrate 35 g; Dietary Fibre 3 g; Cholesterol 80 mg; 1426 kJ (340 Cal)

Use a fork to shred the meat from the barbecued chicken.

Put the mushrooms in a bowl, cover with boiling water and leave to soak.

Cut the noodles into shorter lengths to make them easier to eat.

LEEK AND POTATO SOUP

Preparation time: 15 minutes
Total cooking time: 30 minutes
Serves 4

4 leeks, trimmed and cut into
    4 lengthways
30 g (1 oz) butter
3 floury potatoes, chopped
750 ml (3 cups) chicken or
    vegetable stock
250 ml (1 cup) milk
1/4 teaspoon ground nutmeg
cream and chopped fresh spring
    onions (scallions), to garnish

1 Wash the leeks thoroughly in cold water to remove any dirt, then cut into small chunks. Heat the butter in a large saucepan. Add the leek and cook for 3–4 minutes, stirring frequently, until softened. Add the potato and stock. Bring slowly to the boil, then reduce the heat and simmer for 20 minutes, or until the vegetables are tender.

2 Cool the mixture slightly then transfer to a blender or food processor and purée in batches. Return to the pan, stir in the milk and nutmeg, and season well with salt and ground black pepper. Reheat gently and serve garnished with a swirl of cream and a scattering of spring onion.

NUTRITION PER SERVE
Protein 4 g; Fat 6.5 g; Carbohydrate 16 g; Dietary Fibre 4 g; Cholesterol 20 mg; 584 kJ (140 Cal)

COOK'S FILE

Note: Use old floury potatoes such as sebago for the best results.

Wash the leeks under running water to remove any dirt.

Cook the leek in the butter, stirring frequently, until softened.

Transfer the mixture to a blender or food processor and purée in batches.

PEA AND HAM SOUP

Preparation time: 15 minutes +
  overnight soaking
Total cooking time: 2 hours
Serves 8

500 g (1 lb 2 oz) split peas
1 leek
1 tablespoon oil
2 carrots, chopped
1 celery stalk, chopped
2 garlic cloves, crushed
750 g (1 lb 10 oz) meaty ham
  bone

1 Put the split peas in a large bowl, completely cover with water and soak overnight.

2 Cut the leek in half lengthways and wash thoroughly in cold water to remove any dirt. Slice thickly. Heat the oil in a large saucepan, and add the leek, carrot, celery and garlic. Cook, stirring, for 2–3 minutes, then add the drained peas, the ham bone and 2.5 litres (10 cups) water. Bring to the boil, then reduce the heat and simmer for 2 hours, stirring occasionally.

3 Remove the ham bone and set it aside to cool. Cool the soup a little then purée in batches in a blender or food processor and return to the pan. Remove the meat from the bone, chop and return the meat to the soup. Season to taste with salt and ground black pepper, reheat gently and serve hot.

NUTRITION PER SERVE
Protein 17 g; Fat 8 g; Carbohydrate 8.5 g;
Dietary Fibre 4 g; Cholesterol 30 mg;
725 kJ (175 Cal)

COOK'S FILE

Note: Either yellow or green split peas can be used in this recipe.

Soak the split peas in water overnight, then drain before adding to the soup.

Add the peas, ham bone and water to the pan and bring to the boil.

Remove the meat from the bone and cut into small chunks.

MINESTRONE

Preparation time: 30 minutes
Total cooking time: 2 hours 30 minutes
Serves 8

1 tablespoon olive oil
1 onion, finely chopped
2 garlic cloves, crushed
2 carrots, diced
2 potatoes, diced
2 celery stalks, finely chopped
2 zucchini (courgettes), finely
 chopped
125 g (4¹/₂ oz) green beans,
 chopped
150 g (2 cups) shredded
 cabbage
2 litres (8 cups) beef stock
425 g (15 oz) can chopped
 tomatoes
80 g (¹/₂ cup) macaroni
440 g (1 lb) can borlotti or red
 kidney beans, drained
grated Parmesan cheese, to serve
thyme sprigs, to serve

1 Heat the oil in a large saucepan. Add the onion and garlic and cook over low heat for 5 minutes. Add the carrot, potato and celery and cook, stirring constantly, for a further 5 minutes.

2 Add the zucchini, green beans and cabbage to the pan and cook, stirring, for 5 minutes. Add the stock and chopped tomatoes. Bring slowly to the boil, then reduce the heat, cover and leave to simmer for 2 hours.

3 Add the macaroni and beans, and cook for 15 minutes, or until pasta is tender. Serve hot with a generous sprinkling of Parmesan and garnish with a sprig of fresh thyme.

NUTRITION PER SERVE
Protein 20 g; Fat 4 g; Carbohydrate 55 g; Dietary Fibre 10.5 g; Cholesterol 0 mg; 1320 kJ (314 Cal)

Finely shred the cabbage with a large sharp knife.

Heat the oil in a pan, add the onion and garlic and cook, stirring.

Add the chopped zucchini, beans and shredded cabbage to the pan.

Place the haddock in a frying pan, cover with water and bring to the boil.

Remove the haddock from the pan and drain on paper towels.

Flake the haddock flesh with a fork, discarding the skin and bone.

Add the milk gradually and cook, stirring, until thickened.

SMOKED HADDOCK CHOWDER

Preparation time: 20 minutes
Total cooking time: 25 minutes
Serves 4

500 g (1 lb 2 oz) smoked
   haddock
1 leek, washed and finely
   chopped
1 celery stalk, finely chopped
2 potatoes, diced
50 g (1¾ oz) butter
3 tablespoons plain
   (all-purpose) flour
500 ml (2 cups) milk
60 ml (¼ cup) cream
15 g (¼ cup) chopped parsley

1 Put the haddock in a large deep frying pan and cover with water. Bring to the boil for 1 minute, then drain. Add 500 ml (2 cups) water and bring to the boil, then reduce the heat and simmer for 8 minutes. Remove the fish and drain on paper towels. Reserve the poaching liquid. Let the haddock cool, then flake, discarding the skin and bone. Cover and set aside.
2 Put the leek, celery and potato in a large saucepan. Add the poaching liquid and enough water to make it up to 750 ml (3 cups). Pour into the pan, bring to the boil, then reduce the heat and simmer for 10 minutes.
3 Meanwhile, melt the butter in a saucepan. Add the flour and cook, stirring, for 1 minute. Remove from the heat and gradually add the milk, then cook, stirring, for 2 minutes, or until it boils and thickens. Cook for 2 minutes, then add the cream, fish, vegetables, poaching liquid and parsley. Season to taste with salt and ground black pepper. Reheat without boiling and serve hot.

NUTRITION PER SERVE
Protein 27.5 g; Fat 22 g; Carbohydrate
22 g; Dietary Fibre 2 g; Cholesterol
110 mg; 1600 kJ (381 Cal)

THAI BEEF SOUP

Preparation time: 20 minutes
Total cooking time: 30 minutes
Serves 4

3 tablespoons oil
1 onion, finely chopped
1 teaspoon grated ginger
1 teaspoon grated galangal
2 garlic cloves, crushed
2 stalks lemongrass (white part
    only), finely chopped
4 red chillies, seeds removed,
    finely chopped
4 macadamia nuts, crushed
1 tablespoon Tom Yum paste
2 x 400 g (14 oz) cans coconut
    milk
750 ml (3 cups) beef stock
3 teaspoons sugar
100 g (3¹/₂ oz) green beans,
    halved
1 carrot, julienned
300 g (10¹/₂ oz) fresh Hokkien
    (egg) noodles
100 g (3¹/₂ oz) bean sprouts
55 g (2 oz) thinly sliced cooked
    beef, cut into strips
fresh coriander (cilantro) leaves,
    to garnish

1 Heat the oil in a saucepan, then add the onion, ginger, galangal, garlic, lemongrass, chilli and macadamias. Cook, stirring, over moderate heat for 3–4 minutes, or until the mixture becomes fragrant and changes colour. Add the Tom Yum paste and stir briefly before gradually adding the coconut milk and stock, stirring constantly to mix the paste into the liquid. Add the sugar and ¹/₂ teaspoon salt and bring to the boil. Reduce the heat to low and simmer for 10 minutes. Add the beans and carrot, and cook for 5 minutes more. Skim any fat from the top.
2 Add the noodles, sprouts and beef just before serving, and cook just long enough to heat through. Garnish with coriander leaves. The soup is best eaten with chopsticks and a soup spoon.

NUTRITION PER SERVE
Protein 20 g; Fat 58 g; Carbohydrate 65 g; Dietary Fibre 8.5 g; Cholesterol 25 mg; 3599 kJ (860 Cal)

Peel the galangal and finely grate with a wooden grater.

Wearing protective gloves, remove the seeds and finely chop the chillies.

Use a sharp knife to cut the carrot into julienne strips.

Stir in the onion, ginger, galangal, garlic, lemongrass, chilli and macadamias.

CHUNKY VEGETABLE SOUP

Preparation time: 25 minutes
Total cooking time: 1 hour 30 minutes
Serves 6

50 g (1³/4 oz) butter
1 leek, chopped
1 celery stalk, chopped
1 large carrot, chopped
1 large potato, chopped
1 parsnip, peeled and
   chopped
1 swede (rutabaga) or turnip,
   peeled and chopped

225 g (8 oz) sweet potato,
   chopped
115 g (¹/2 cup) soup mix
2 litres (8 cups) vegetable stock
   or water
155 g (1 cup) frozen peas
125 g (4¹/2 oz) green beans,
   chopped
15 g (¹/4 cup) chopped mint
20 g (¹/3 cup) chopped parsley

1 Heat the butter in a large saucepan, and cook the leek, celery, carrot, potato, parsnip, swede or turnip and sweet potato, stirring, for 5 minutes.
2 Add the soup mix and stock or water. Bring slowly to the boil, then reduce the heat and simmer, covered, for 1¹/4 hours, or until the soup mix has softened.
3 Add the peas and beans, and cook for a further 10 minutes, or until tender. Stir in the chopped mint and parsley. Season to taste and serve hot. Delicious with crusty bread.

NUTRITION PER SERVE
Protein 3 g; Fat 7 g; Carbohydrate 15 g;
Dietary Fibre 4 g; Cholesterol 20 mg;
555 kJ (135 Cal)

COOK'S FILE

Note: Soup mix is a combination of dried beans and pulses.

Measure 115 g (¹/2 cup) of the soup mix before adding to the vegetables.

Top and tail the beans, then chop them into short lengths.

Add the soup mix and stock or water and slowly bring to the boil.

WELSH RAREBIT

Preparation time: 5 minutes
Total cooking time: 10 minutes
Serves 4

120 g (4¹/₂ oz) strong cheese
30 g (1 oz) butter, softened
2 teaspoons English mustard
1 egg, beaten
1 tablespoon beer (Guinness
    or stout)

1 teaspoon Worcestershire
    sauce
6 slices bread

1 Grate the cheese on the fine side of the cheese grater, and combine with the butter, mustard, egg, beer and Worcestershire sauce. Season with salt and ground black pepper.
2 Toast the bread on both sides and then spread one side of each piece with a layer of the cheese mixture, dividing the mixture evenly among the slices. Make sure the toast is covered right up to the edges. Grill (broil) under a hot grill (broiler) until browned and bubbling. Serve as a snack or with a salad as a light lunch, and wash down with the remainder of the Guinness.

NUTRITION PER SERVE
Protein 12 g; Fat 15 g; Carbohydrate 20 g; Dietary Fibre 1 g; Cholesterol 80 mg; 1065 kJ (255 Cal)

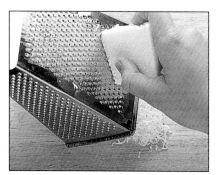

Finely grate the cheese on the fine side of a cheese grater.

Combine the cheese, butter, mustard, egg, beer and Worcestershire sauce.

Spread the cheese mixture evenly over each slice of toast.

SCRAMBLED EGGS

Preparation time: 5 minutes
Total cooking time: 5 minutes
Serves 2

6 eggs
1 tablespoon milk or cream
50 g (1¾ oz) butter
2 slices toast

1 Crack the eggs into a bowl, add the milk or cream and season well, to taste, with salt and ground black pepper. Whisk gently with a fork.
2 Melt half the butter in a small pan or frying pan over low heat. Add the eggs, and stir constantly with a wooden spoon. Do not turn up the heat—scrambling must be done slowly and gently. When most of the egg has set, add the remaining butter and remove the pan from the heat. There should be enough heat left in the pan to finish cooking the eggs and melt the butter. Scrambled eggs should be creamy, not dry or rubbery. Serve immediately on toast—they will not sit even for a minute.

NUTRITION PER SERVE
Protein 20 g; Fat 35 g; Carbohydrate 15 g; Dietary Fibre 1 g; Cholesterol 605 mg; 1935 kJ (460 Cal)

COOK'S FILE

Note: It is very important to use fresh eggs when scrambling. To check whether an egg is fresh put it in a bowl of cold water: if it sinks on its side it is fresh, and if it floats on its end it is stale. If it is somewhere between the two it is not perfectly fresh but still usable.
Variations: Scrambled eggs are also delicious with cheese such as Gruyère stirred through them, or smoked salmon pieces or bacon with some of your favourite herbs. You could add roasted vegetables such as capsicum (pepper), tomato, onion and fresh basil to make Piperade.

Break up the eggs with a fork and stir gently until well combined.

Pour in the eggs and stir constantly with a wooden spoon.

When the eggs are nearly set, add the butter and remove from the heat.

LIGHT AND FLUFFY OMELETTES

Preparation time: 5 minutes
Total cooking time: 5 minutes
Serves 1

3 eggs
10 g (1/4 oz) butter
1/2 teaspoon oil

1 Crack the eggs into a small bowl and add a teaspoon of water. Break them up with a fork but do not overbeat them—the yolk and white should be just combined. Season well.
2 Melt the butter and oil in a non-stick or well-seasoned frying pan. A 15 cm (6 inch) diameter is about the right size for 3 eggs. When the butter has melted, swirl it around the pan, turn up the heat and pour in the egg.
3 Tilt the pan to cover the base with egg and leave it for a few seconds. Using a spatula or egg flip draw the sides of the omelette into the centre and let any extra liquid egg run to the outside. As soon as the egg is almost set, tip the pan on a 45-degree angle and flip one half of the omelette into the middle and then over again so you have a flatish roll. Slide the omelette onto a plate and eat immediately. The egg will continue cooking inside the omelette.

NUTRITION PER SERVE
Protein 18 g; Fat 28 g; Carbohydrate 0.5 g; Dietary Fibre 0 g; Cholesterol 565 mg; 1345 kJ (320 Cal)

COOK'S FILE

Note: If you are making omelettes for more than one person make each one separately. For the best results, use very fresh eggs.
Variation: Make a meal of your omelette by adding 50 g (1 3/4 oz) shredded smoked salmon or 30 g (1 oz) grated tasty cheese.

Gently break up the eggs with a fork but do not overbeat them.

Draw the sides of the omelette in so that any liquid egg flows to the outside.

When the egg is almost set, flip half of the omelette into the middle.

FRITTATA

Preparation time: 15 minutes
Total cooking time: 25 minutes
Serves 4

60 g (2¹/4 oz) green beans, cut
　　into short lengths
80 g (¹/2 cup) frozen peas
1 carrot, chopped
5 eggs
3 tablespoons olive oil
1 large red onion, sliced
1 garlic clove, crushed
4 spring onions (scallions),
　　sliced

2 rashers back bacon, chopped
1 cooked potato, cut into
　　even-sized pieces
1 tablespoon parsley, chopped

1 Bring a saucepan of water to the
boil. Add the beans, peas and carrot,
and cook for 5 minutes.
2 Put the eggs in a bowl and beat
together until well mixed. Season with
salt and ground black pepper.
3 In a non-stick frying pan with a
handle suitable for using under a grill
(broiler), heat the oil and add the
onion and garlic. Cook, stirring, for
3–4 minutes, then add the spring
onion and bacon and continue cooking
until the bacon is cooked.

4 Add the beans, peas, carrot and
potato and stir with a wooden spoon
to evenly distribute over the pan. Pour
the eggs into the pan and tip it from
side to side until you have an even
layer of egg. Cook over low heat for
10–12 minutes, or until the base is
browned and the top is just set.
Remove the pan from the heat
and put under a hot grill (broiler) until
the top is well browned. Either invert
the frittata onto a plate or slide it out
and sprinkle with parsley before
cutting into wedges. Serve with a salad.

NUTRITION PER SERVE
Protein 14 g; Fat 20 g; Carbohydrate 8 g;
Dietary Fibre 4 g; Cholesterol 235 mg;
1180 kJ (280 Cal)

*Add the beans, peas and carrot to the
boiling water and cook until tender.*

*Cook the red onion, spring onion and
bacon until the bacon is cooked.*

*Tip the pan from side to side until the
egg is evenly distributed.*

Jaffles

Jaffles can be as simple or as full of flavour as your imagination (or hunger!) dictates. Some old favourites will always endure but use the wide range of sun-dried (sun-blushed) vegetables, cheeses and cold meats readily available at your local deli or supermarket, to make something really special.

EGG, HAM AND CHEESE

Butter a slice of bread and gently press, butter-side down, onto the base of a lightly greased preheated jaffle maker. Crack an egg onto the bread and top with sliced ham and grated cheese. Top with a slice of buttered bread, butter-side-up, and cook until golden.

ROAST BEEF AND CAMEMBERT

Butter a slice of bread and gently press, butter-side down, onto the base of a lightly greased preheated jaffle maker. Spread on some mustard, and top with sliced roast beef, some camembert and baby English spinach leaves. Top with a second buttered slice of bread, butter-side up, and cook until golden brown.

CORN AND TUNA

Butter a slice of bread and place, butter-side down, in a lightly greased preheated jaffle maker. Spread with a couple of spoonfuls of creamed corn, then add some drained tuna in oil, two slices of tasty Cheddar and chopped spring onion (scallion). Top with a buttered slice of bread, butter-side-up, and cook until golden.

BAKED BEANS AND CHEESE

Butter a slice of bread and place, butter-side down, in a lightly greased preheated jaffle maker. Top with 2 slices of tasty Cheddar then spread with 2 tablespoons canned baked beans. Top with a second buttered slice of bread, butter-side up, and cook until golden brown.

CHICKEN, PESTO AND SUN-DRIED TOMATO

Cut a focaccia breadroll in half and butter both sides. Place one half, butter-side up, in a lightly greased preheated jaffle maker. Spread some good-quality bought pesto over the bread, then add a couple of slices of Swiss cheese, some chopped sun-dried (sun-blushed) tomatoes and a few slices of cooked chicken breast. Cover with the other half of the breadroll, butter-side down, and cook until golden brown.

APPLE AND CINNAMON

Butter a slice of bread, sprinkle with a mixture of sugar and cinnamon and place, butter-side down, in a lightly greased preheated jaffle maker. Combine a small can of apple purée with a tablespoon of sultanas, a pinch of cinnamon and a little sugar, and spread onto the bread, finishing with a second slice of buttered bread, butter-side-up. Sprinkle with sugar and cinnamon and cook until golden brown. Serve with custard.

VEGETARIAN

Cut a piece of Turkish bread in half and lightly butter both sides. Place one half of the bread, butter-side up, in a lightly greased preheated jaffle maker. Spread a little bottled tomato salsa over the bread, then spread on some cooked mashed sweet potato. Top with thin strips of roasted red capsicum (pepper), some crumbled feta cheese and a few baby English spinach leaves. Cover with the other half of the Turkish bread, butter-side-down, and cook until golden brown.

BANANA AND MAPLE SYRUP

Butter a slice of bread and place, butter-side down, in a lightly greased preheated jaffle maker. Mash a banana with 1 tablespoon maple syrup and spread on the bread. Sprinkle on a few chopped pecans or walnuts and top with a second slice of bread, butter-side up, and cook until golden brown.

From left to right: Vegetarian; Chicken, pesto and sun-dried tomato; Apple and cinnamon; Banana and maple syrup; Egg, ham and cheese; Baked beans and cheese; Roast beef and camembert; Corn and tuna

NACHOS

Preparation time: 25 minutes
Total cooking time: 10 minutes
Serves 4

3 tomatoes, diced
1 small red onion, finely
  chopped
3 tablespoons chopped fresh
  coriander (cilantro) leaves
1 tablespoon lime juice
1 garlic clove, crushed
1 small red chilli, deseeded
  and finely chopped
400 g (14 oz) can red kidney
  beans
200 g (7 oz) jar taco sauce
230 g (8 oz) packet corn chips
250 g (2 cups) grated cheese
1 avocado
sour cream, to serve

1 Preheat the oven to 180°C (350°F/ Gas 4). Combine the tomato, onion, coriander, lime juice, garlic and chilli in a bowl, then cover and set aside to let the flavours combine.
2 Rinse and drain the kidney beans, then put them in a small saucepan with the taco sauce and stir until the sauce boils and the beans are heated through. Divide among four ovenproof plates, keeping the mixture towards the centre of the plate.
3 Arrange the corn chips around the beans. Sprinkle the beans with cheese, and bake for 5 minutes, or until the cheese has melted. Meanwhile, peel and dice the avocado, and fold gently through the tomato salsa.
4 Spoon the salsa on top of the nachos, and serve with sour cream on the side. Serve immediately.

NUTRITION PER SERVE
Protein 30 g; Fat 45 g; Carbohydrate 50 g; Dietary Fibre 15 g; Cholesterol 70 mg; 3095 kJ (740 Cal)

COOK'S FILE

Variation: For beef nachos, cook lean minced (ground) beef in a little oil over medium heat until browned and cooked through. Stir the beef through with the beans and taco sauce and serve as above.

Wearing protective gloves, deseed and finely chop the chilli.

Mix together the tomato, onion, coriander, lime juice, garlic and chilli.

QUICHE LORRAINE

Preparation time: 35 minutes + chilling
Total cooking time: 1 hour 5 minutes
Serves 6

155 g (1¼ cups) plain
 (all-purpose) flour
90 g (3¼ oz) cold butter,
 chopped
2–3 tablespoons iced water
4 rashers streaky bacon
75 g (2½ oz) Gruyère cheese,
 grated
3 eggs
125 ml (½ cup) cream
125 ml (½ cup) milk

1 Sift the flour into a bowl and rub in the butter with your fingertips until the mixture resembles fine breadcrumbs. Make a well in the centre and add the water. Using a cutting action, mix with a flat-bladed knife until the mixture comes together. Gently gather the dough together and lift onto a floured surface. Press into a ball and flatten it slightly. Wrap in plastic wrap and refrigerate for 15 minutes. Preheat the oven to 200°C (400°F/Gas 6).

2 Roll the dough out between two sheets of baking paper to fit a 23 cm (9 inch) fluted flan tin. Remove the top sheet of paper and invert the pastry into the tin. Use a small ball of pastry to press the pastry into the tin, leaving any excess to hang over the sides. Roll the rolling pin over the tin to cut off any excess, and refrigerate for 15 minutes.

3 Line the pastry shell with a sheet of crumpled greaseproof paper. Pour in some baking beads and bake for 15 minutes. Remove the paper and beads and return the pastry to the oven for 10 minutes, or until the base is dry. Cool completely before filling. Reduce the oven to 180°C (350°F/Gas 4).

4 Finely chop the bacon and cook in a frying pan until brown and crisp. Drain, then spread over the pastry base. Sprinkle the cheese over the bacon. In a jug, whisk together the eggs, cream and milk. Stand the flan tin on a baking tray, and pour the egg mixture into the pastry shell. Bake for 35–40 minutes, or until set and golden.

NUTRITION PER SERVE
Protein 15 g; Fat 28 g; Carbohydrate 20 g; Dietary Fibre 1 g; Cholesterol 180 mg; 1640 kJ (390 Cal)

Add the water and mix together with a flat-bladed knife.

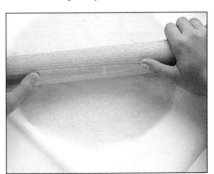

Roll out the dough until it is large enough to line the tin.

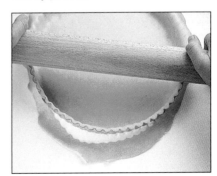

Remove any excess pastry by rolling a rolling pin over the top of the tin.

CAULIFLOWER CHEESE

Preparation time: 15 minutes
Total cooking time: 20 minutes
Serves 4

500 g (1 lb 2 oz) cauliflower,
   cut into pieces
30 g (1 oz) butter
30 g (1 oz) plain (all-purpose)
   flour
315 ml (1¼ cups) warm milk
1 teaspoon Dijon mustard
60 g (½ cup) grated Cheddar
   cheese
50 g (½ cup) grated Parmesan
   cheese
2 tablespoons fresh breadcrumbs

3 tablespoons grated Cheddar,
extra

1 Grease a 1.5 litre (6 cup) heatproof dish. Cook the cauliflower in lightly salted boiling water until just tender. Drain. Put in the dish and keep warm.
2 Melt the butter in a pan. Stir in the flour and cook for 1 minute, or until golden and bubbling. Remove from heat; whisk in the milk and mustard. Return to heat and bring to the boil, stirring constantly. Cook, stirring, over low heat for 2 minutes. Remove from the heat; add the cheeses and stir until melted. Do not reheat the sauce or the oil will come out of the cheese. Season and pour over the cauliflower.
3 Combine the breadcrumbs and extra cheese and sprinkle over the

sauce. Grill (broil) until top is browned and bubbling. Serve immediately.

NUTRITION PER SERVE
Protein 22 g; Fat 33 g; Carbohydrate 15 g;
Dietary Fibre 2 g; Cholesterol 88 mg;
1840 kJ (440 Cal)

Add the Cheddar and Parmesan and stir until the cheeses have melted.

MACARONI CHEESE BAKE

Preparation time: 15 minutes
Total cooking time: 35 minutes
Serves 4

225 g (8 oz) macaroni
80 g (3oz) butter
1 onion, finely chopped
3 tablespoons plain (all-purpose)
    flour
500 ml (2 cups) milk
2 teaspoons wholegrain mustard
150 g (5½ oz) vintage Cheddar
    cheese, grated
100 g (3½ oz) Cheddar cheese,
    grated
30 g (1 oz) fresh breadcrumbs

1 Cook the pasta in a saucepan of boiling salted water until just tender. Drain well.
2 Preheat the oven to 180°C (350°F/ Gas 4) and grease a 1.5 litre (6 cup) ovenproof dish.
3 Melt the butter in a large frying pan over low heat, add the onion and cook for 5 minutes. Stir in the flour and cook for 1 minute, or until pale and foaming. Remove from the heat and gradually stir in the milk. Return to the heat and stir until the sauce boils and thickens. Reduce the heat and simmer for 2 minutes. Stir in the mustard and three-quarters of the combined cheeses. Season to taste. Add the pasta to the pan and mix well. Spoon into the dish.
4 Combine the breadcrumbs and remaining cheese and scatter over the top. Bake for about 15 minutes, or until golden brown and bubbling.

NUTRITION PER SERVE
Protein 30 g; Fat 45 g; Carbohydrate 60 g; Dietary Fibre 4 g; Cholesterol 130 mg; 3087 kJ (737 Cal)

Cook the onion in the butter over medium heat until softened.

CHEESE SOUFFLE

Preparation time: 10 minutes
Total cooking time: 35 minutes
Serves 4

60 g (2¼ oz) butter
45 g (1½ oz) plain (all-purpose) flour
315 ml (1¼ cups) milk, warmed
185 g (1½ cups) grated Cheddar cheese, firmly packed
1 teaspoon Dijon mustard
4 eggs, separated
1 tablespoon grated Parmesan cheese

1 Preheat the oven to 200°C (400°F/Gas 6). Brush a 1.5 litre (6 cup) soufflé dish with melted butter or oil. Melt the butter in a large pan then add the flour. Stir over low heat for 2 minutes, or until the flour is lightly golden and bubbling. Remove from the heat and gradually add the milk, stirring until the mixture is smooth. Return the pan to the heat and stir constantly over low heat until the mixture boils and thickens. Simmer for 1 minute, then remove from the heat.
2 Add the Cheddar, Dijon mustard and egg yolks, and stir until the cheese has melted. Season to taste with salt and ground black pepper. Cover the surface with plastic wrap and leave the sauce to cool slightly.
3 Put the egg whites in a clean dry bowl and whisk until stiff peaks form. Using a metal spoon, fold one third of the egg whites into the sauce, then gently fold in the remaining egg whites, being careful not to lose any volume. Gently pour the mixture into the prepared dish. Run your thumb or a knife around the edge of the dish to push the soufflé mixture slightly away from the edge—this will help it to rise evenly.
4 Sprinkle with the Parmesan and bake the soufflé for 25–30 minutes, or until well risen and cooked through (cover it if it appears to be over-browning). Serve immediately with a green salad.

NUTRITION PER SERVE
Protein 30 g; Fat 50 g; Carbohydrate 15 g; Dietary Fibre 0.5 g; Cholesterol 365 mg; 2655 kJ (635 Cal)

Lightly brush the soufflé dish with melted butter or oil.

Gently fold the egg whites into the sauce with a metal spoon.

Run your thumb around the edge of the soufflé dish.

BUBBLE AND SQUEAK

Preparation time: 15 minutes
Total cooking time: 30 minutes
Serves 4

750 g (1 lb 10 oz) floury potatoes
125 ml (½ cup) milk
80 g (3 oz) butter
450 g (1 lb) green vegetables (such as cabbage, leek, Brussels sprouts, English spinach), finely sliced

1 Cut the potatoes into even-sized pieces and put them in a pan of cold water. Bring to the boil, then lower the heat and simmer until tender—do not boil or the potatoes may break up and absorb water before they cook through. Drain well.
2 Heat the milk in the pan. Add the potatoes and half of the butter, then mash with a potato masher or beat with electric beaters until the mixture is smooth and creamy.
3 Melt half of the remaining butter in a large frying pan with a handle suitable for using under a grill (broiler), and cook the green vegetables until they are tender. Add them to the potato and mix together. Season to taste with salt and ground black pepper.
4 Melt the remaining butter in the frying pan and spoon in the potato mixture, smoothing off the top, and cook until the bottom is browned and crispy. Remove the pan from the heat and place it under a preheated grill (broiler) until the top is browned and golden. If you prefer, turn the bubble and squeak over in the pan and cook on the other side, but grilling is easier. This can be served as a side dish or a main meal with gravy.

NUTRITION PER SERVE
Protein 7 g; Fat 18 g; Carbohydrate 30 g; Dietary Fibre 5.5 g; Cholesterol 55 mg; 1280 kJ (305 Cal)

C O O K ' S   F I L E

Variation: Bubble and squeak can be made up with virtually any leftovers, or add a few rashers of bacon or ham.

Add the green vegetables to the pan and cook until tender.

Cheese soufflé (top)
and Bubble and squeak

POTATO GRATIN

Preparation time: 25 minutes
Total cooking time: 1 hour 5 minutes +
　10 minutes standing
Serves 4

25 g (1 oz) butter
1 onion, halved and thinly sliced
650 g (1 lb 7 oz) floury
　potatoes, thinly sliced
85 g (2/3 cup) grated Cheddar
　cheese
300 ml (1 carton) cream
100 ml (3 fl oz) milk

1 Heat the butter in a frying pan, add the onion and cook over low heat for 5 minutes, or until it is soft and translucent.
2 Preheat the oven to 160°C (315°F/ Gas 3). Grease the base and sides of a deep 1 litre (4 cup) ovenproof dish. Layer in the potato slices with the onion and cheese (reserving 2 tablespoons of cheese for the top). Whisk together the cream and milk, and season with salt and freshly ground black pepper. Slowly pour over the potato, then sprinkle on the remaining cheese.
3 Bake for 50–60 minutes, or until golden brown and the potato is very soft. Leave for 10 minutes before serving.

NUTRITION PER SERVE
Protein 12 g; Fat 50 g; Carbohydrate 25 g;
Dietary Fibre 3 g; Cholesterol 155 mg;
2465 kJ (590 Cal)

COOK'S FILE

Variation: Try combining potato and orange sweet potato, layering alternately. For extra flavour, add some chopped fresh herbs.

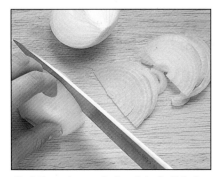

Peel the onion and slice it in half before cutting into thin slices.

Use a large sharp knife to cut the potatoes into thin slices.

Add the onion to the butter and cook until soft and translucent.

LIGHTLY SPICED KEDGEREE

Preparation time: 40 minutes
Total cooking time: 30 minutes
Serves 4

375 g (13 oz) smoked cod
2 bay leaves
3 slices lemon
3 eggs
90 g (3¼ oz) butter
1 onion, finely chopped
½ teaspoon mild Indian curry paste
½ teaspoon ground cumin
550 g (3 cups) cooked cold long-grain rice

2 tablespoons chopped parsley
2 tablespoons lemon juice
125 ml (½ cup) cream

1 Put the cod in a frying pan with the bay leaves and lemon. Cover with cold water. Simmer for about 8 minutes, or until the fish flakes easily when tested with a fork. Remove the fish, drain and cool. Flake into bite-sized pieces.
2 Put the eggs in a pan of water. Bring to the boil and cook for 8–10 minutes, or until hard boiled. Remove. Run under cold water to cool, then peel and chop.
3 Melt the butter in a large deep frying pan, and heat for 2 minutes, or until foaming. Add the onion, curry paste and cumin and cook, stirring, for 4 minutes. Add the rice, fish, parsley and juice. Cook over medium heat for 3 minutes, or until heated through, tossing regularly with two wooden spoons. Add the cream and half the egg. Toss gently.
4 Garnish with the remaining egg and a little parsley. Serve with toast.

NUTRITION PER SERVE
Protein 33 g; Fat 37 g; Carbohydrate 110 g; Dietary Fibre 4 g; Cholesterol 280 mg; 3830 kJ (914 Cal)

COOK'S FILE

Note: For a less spicy flavour, add 1 teaspoon grated lemon zest and ¼ teaspoon ground nutmeg instead of the curry paste and cumin.

Place the cod in a frying pan with the bay leaves and lemon and cover with water.

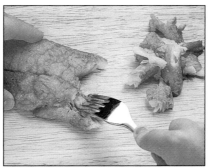

Use a fork to flake the cooled cod into bite-size pieces.

Add the onion, curry paste and cumin to the butter.

TOAD IN THE HOLE

Preparation time: 3 minutes +
30 minutes resting
Total cooking time: 30 minutes
Serves 6

110 g (4 oz) plain (all-purpose)
flour
2 eggs
150 ml (5 fl oz) milk
4–6 large good-quality sausages
60 ml (¹/₄ cup) oil

1 Sift the flour and a pinch of salt into a large bowl and make a well in the centre. Combine the eggs with the milk and 150 ml (5 fl oz) water and add gradually to the flour, mixing constantly until the batter is smooth and lump free. Cover and leave the batter to rest in the refrigerator for half an hour.

2 Preheat the oven to 220°C (425°F/ Gas 7). Fry the sausages in 1 tablespoon of the oil until browned all over but not cooked through. Set aside. Put the rest of the oil in an 18 x 24 cm (7 x 9 inch) ovenproof dish and heat it either on the stove top or in the oven until the oil is smoking hot. The oil must be really hot or the batter will not rise properly.

3 When the oil is hot enough, carefully pour in the batter and add the sausages, spacing them out well so the batter will rise between them. Bake for 20 minutes, or until the batter is well risen and browned. Serve with gravy, steamed beans and grilled tomato.

NUTRITION PER SERVE
Protein 12 g; Fat 27 g; Carbohydrate 16 g; Dietary Fibre 2 g; Cholesterol 93 mg; 1475 kJ (350 Cal)

Stir the batter constantly until smooth and lump free.

When the oil is hot, carefully pour the batter into the dish.

Space the sausages out well so the batter will rise between them.

STUFFED CAPSICUMS WITH TOMATO SAUCE

Preparation time: 25 minutes
Total cooking time: 1 hour 20 minutes
Serves 4

4 red capsicums (peppers)
1 tablespoon oil
1 leek, thinly sliced
2 garlic cloves, crushed
400 g (14 oz) minced (ground) beef
2 x 440 g (15¼ oz) cans crushed tomatoes
250 ml (1 cup) beef stock
45 g (¼ cup) brown lentils
1 potato, cut into small cubes
2 tablespoons tomato paste (purée)
15 g (¼ cup) chopped parsley
15 g (¼ cup) chopped basil
60 ml (¼ cup) red wine
½ teaspoon caster (superfine) sugar
1 bay leaf
40 g (½ cup) fresh breadcrumbs
1 tablespoon butter, melted
2 teaspoons finely chopped parsley, extra

1 Slice off the stalk end of the capsicums and remove the seeds and membranes. Cut a thin slice off the base of each capsicum so they sit flat.
2 Heat the oil in a pan, add the leek and garlic and stir over medium heat for about 5 minutes, or until the leek is just soft. Add the beef and cook until browned all over.
3 Add one can of tomatoes, the stock, lentils, potato and half the tomato paste. Bring to the boil, then reduce the heat and simmer for 30 minutes, or until the vegetables are tender and the mixture is thick. Stir in the herbs and season.
4 Preheat the oven to 180°C (350°F/

Gas 4). Spoon the mixture into the capsicums and put them in a shallow ovenproof dish. Heat the remaining can of tomatoes, tomato paste, wine, sugar and bay leaf in a small pan, season to taste and then spoon around the capsicums.
5 Sprinkle the capsicums with the combined breadcrumbs, butter and parsley. Put the capsicum lids in the baking dish. Bake for 30 minutes, or until crisp on top. Put the lids on the capsicums and serve.

NUTRITION PER SERVE
Protein 30 g; Fat 20 g; Carbohydrate 30 g; Dietary Fibre 8.5 g; Cholesterol 75 mg; 1820 kJ (435 Cal)

With a small sharp knife, carefully remove the seeds and membranes.

Spoon the stuffing mixture into the prepared capsicums.

Potatoes

There's something very friendly about baked potatoes. Delicious with just a knob of butter and a little ground pepper, or a mouth-watering topping, they are the embodiment of comfort food.

BAKED POTATOES

Preheat the oven to 220°C (425°F/Gas 7). Wash and dry large potatoes and prick them several times with a fork. Brush the potatoes with a little oil and place them on a baking tray. Bake for 1–1½ hours, or until tender when tested with a skewer.

ROASTED POTATO SHELLS

Boil or steam potatoes for 10–15 minutes, or until just tender when tested with a skewer (be careful not to overcook). Drain and leave to cool then cut the potatoes in half and scoop out the flesh leaving a thin border. Preheat the oven to 200°C (400°F/Gas 6). Lightly brush the potato halves with oil, place on baking trays and bake in the oven for 30–45 minutes, or until crisp and golden.

Note: We have used baked potatoes but potato shells work just as well with all the toppings.

TOPPINGS

Grilled garlic field mushrooms

Slice 2 or 3 large field mushrooms into large pieces. Heat 40 g (1½ oz) butter in a heavy-based frying pan and add 1 crushed garlic clove. Cook for 30 seconds, then add the mushrooms and cook, tossing, until tender. Add 1 teaspoon chopped fresh parsley and spoon into each potato. Top with a dollop of sour cream and a sprinkle of ground black pepper. Serves 4.

Roasted ratatouille

Chop ½ red capsicum (pepper), 1 zucchini (courgette), ½ medium eggplant (aubergine), 2 tomatoes and 1 small red onion into even-sized pieces. Toss in a bowl with 1 crushed garlic clove and a little olive oil. Season to taste. Put in a baking dish and bake with the potatoes for 30 minutes, or until tender. Spoon into each baked potato and top with grated cheese. Serves 4.

From left to right: Chickpea purée; Crispy bacon and fried egg; Grilled garlic field mushrooms; Chicken and roasted corn salsa; Seafood mornay; Roasted ratatouille

Seafood mornay

Melt 1 tablespoon butter in a small pan, add 1 tablespoon plain (all-purpose) flour and stir it into the butter. Cook for 1 minute, or until pale and foaming, then remove from the heat and gradually stir in 250 ml (1 cup) milk. Return the pan to the heat and stir constantly until the sauce boils and thickens. Simmer for 2 minutes, then turn off the heat and stir in 30 g (1/4 cup) grated cheese. Place 2 tablespoons cooked chopped peeled prawns (shrimp) or canned tuna in each baked potato and top with the sauce. Garnish with some sliced spring onions (scallions). Serves 4.

Crispy bacon and fried egg

Cut 2 rashers streaky bacon into thin strips and fry until crispy then set aside. Fry 2 eggs in the same frying pan until firm, then remove with a spatula. Place a fried egg in each potato and top with the crispy bacon strips. Serve with tomato or Worcestershire sauce. Serves 2.

Chicken and roasted corn salsa

Put 1 corn cob brushed with butter under a hot grill (broiler) and roast, turning so all sides are coloured and cooked through. Slice off the kernels and put them into a bowl with 1 chopped tomato, 1 tablespoon lemon juice, 1 chopped avocado and a few drops of Tabasco. Season and mix well. Cut 1 smoked chicken breast into cubes and add to the salsa. Spoon into baked potatoes. Sprinkle with chopped flat-leaf (Italian) parsley. Serves 4.

Chickpea purée

Put a 400 g (14 oz) can drained chickpeas in a food processor with 1 tablespoon oil, 1 chopped spring onion (scallion), 1 tablespoon lime juice, 1 crushed garlic clove and 1 small deseeded chilli. Blend until you have a smooth paste. Stir through 1 chopped tomato, 1 tablespoon sour cream and 1 tablespoon chopped coriander (cilantro). Spoon into baked potatoes and serve with extra lime to squeeze over. Serves 4.

75

FRIED RICE

Preparation time: 25 minutes +
  30 minutes soaking
Total cooking time: 20 minutes
Serves 4

2 dried Chinese mushrooms
2 tablespoons peanut oil
2 eggs, well beaten
4 rashers back bacon, chopped
2 teaspoons finely grated
  ginger
1 garlic clove, finely chopped
6 spring onions (scallions),
  finely chopped
1 teaspoon sesame oil
750 g (4 cups) cooked, cold
  long-grain white rice
150 g (5¹/2 oz) frozen peas,
  thawed
50 g (1³/4 oz) water chestnuts,
  chopped

100 g (3¹/2 oz) cooked, peeled,
  small prawns (shrimp)
2 tablespoons soy sauce

1 Soak the mushrooms in boiling water for 30 minutes. Drain and finely slice, discarding the stalks.
2 Heat a large wok until very hot, add about 2 teaspoons of the peanut oil and swirl. Pour in the eggs and scramble until they are just cooked. Remove from the wok and set aside. Reheat the wok and stir-fry the bacon for 2 minutes. Add the ginger, garlic and spring onion and stir-fry for 1 minute. Remove from the wok.
3 Reheat the wok to smoking hot, add the sesame oil, the remaining peanut oil and the rice. Stir-fry, tossing regularly, until the rice is heated through.
4 Add the egg, bacon mixture, peas, water chestnuts, prawns and mushrooms to the wok and toss well.

Cover and steam for 1 minute, or until everything is heated through. Stir in the soy sauce and season well with salt and ground black pepper.

NUTRITION PER SERVE
Protein 20 g; Fat 15 g; Carbohydrate 5 g;
Dietary Fibre 3 g; Cholesterol 0 mg;
1075 kJ (255 Cal)

Cover the mushrooms with boiling water and leave to soak for 30 minutes.

FETTUCINE CARBONARA

Preparation time: 10 minutes
Total cooking time: 25 minutes
Serves 4

500 g (1 lb 2 oz) fettucine
3 eggs, lightly beaten
125 ml (1/2 cup) cream
35 g (1/3 cup) finely grated
   Parmesan cheese
20 g (1 oz) butter
250 g (9 oz) streaky bacon,
   cut into thin strips
2 garlic cloves, crushed
4 spring onions (scallions),
   finely chopped

1 Bring a large saucepan of water to the boil, add the pasta and cook for 10–12 minutes, or until just tender.
2 Whisk together the eggs, cream and Parmesan and season with salt and ground black pepper.
3 Meanwhile, melt the butter in a frying pan, add the bacon strips and cook for 5–8 minutes, or until lightly golden. Add the garlic and spring onion and cook for 2–3 minutes. Remove from the heat.
4 Drain the pasta, and transfer to a large serving bowl. While the pasta is still hot pour in the egg mixture and toss well to combine (the heat from the pasta should be sufficient to cook the egg). Add the bacon mixture and toss through. Season to taste and serve immediately.

NUTRITION PER SERVE
Protein 35 g; Fat 30 g; Carbohydrate 90 g; Dietary Fibre 6.5 g; Cholesterol 235 mg; 3213 kJ (765 Cal)

Whisk together the eggs, cream, cheese, salt and pepper.

Pour the egg mixture over the hot pasta and toss to combine.

BLUE CHEESE GNOCCHI

Preparation time: 20 minutes
Total cooking time: 20 minutes
Serves 4

500 g (1 lb 2 oz) potatoes,
  quartered
155 g (1¼ cups) plain
  (all-purpose) flour

Sauce
300 ml (1 carton) cream
125 g (4½ oz) gorgonzola
  cheese, roughly chopped
2 tablespoons chopped chives

1 Cook the potatoes in boiling salted water for 15–20 minutes, or in the microwave until tender. Salt generously. Drain the potatoes then mash until completely smooth. Transfer to a bowl.

2 Sprinkle the flour into the bowl with one hand while kneading it into the potato mixture with the other hand. Continue kneading until all the flour is worked in and the dough is smooth.

3 Divide the dough into three and roll each portion into a sausage that is 2 cm (³/₄ inch) thick. Cut into 2.5 cm (1 inch) lengths and, using floured hands, press each gnocchi against a fork to flatten it and indent one side (the indentation helps the sauce stick to the cooked gnocchi).

4 Bring a large saucepan of water to the boil. When rapidly boiling, drop in the gnocchi, then reduce the heat and simmer for 2–3 minutes, or until the gnocchi rise to the surface. Remove the gnocchi with a slotted spoon and drain well. Put on a serving dish and keep warm.

5 Put the cream into a small pan and bring to the boil. Boil rapidly, stirring constantly, for about 5 minutes, or until the sauce has reduced by one third. Remove from the heat and stir through the cheese. Season with salt and pepper, and pour over the gnocchi. Scatter the chives over the top and serve immediately.

NUTRITION PER SERVE
Protein 20 g; Fat 45 g; Carbohydrate 45 g; Dietary Fibre 3.5 g; Cholesterol 130 mg; 2736 kJ (655 Cal)

Add the flour with one hand while kneading it into the potato with the other.

Gently knead the mixture until all the flour is mixed in and the dough is smooth.

Press the gnocchi against a fork to flatten it and indent one side.

Drop the gnocchi into boiling water and simmer until they rise.

ROMAN GNOCCHI

Preparation time: 20 minutes +
    45 minutes freezing time
Total cooking time: 35 minutes
Serves 4

750 ml (3 cups) milk
20 g (1 oz) butter
pinch nutmeg
90 g (³/4 cup) semolina
2 eggs, lightly beaten
135 g (1¹/3 cups) grated
    Parmesan cheeese
30 g (1 cup) shredded basil
    leaves
2 tablespoons pine nuts, toasted
50 g (1³/4 oz) butter, melted

1 teaspoon white wine vinegar
4 Roma (plum) tomatoes, sliced

1 Put the milk, butter and nutmeg in a large pan and bring to the boil. In a thin stream, slowly pour the semolina into the milk, stirring constantly. Cook, stirring, over low heat for 12–13 minutes, or until very thick. Remove from the heat, stir in the eggs and 125 g (1¹/4 cups) of the Parmesan and season well.
2 Spoon onto a 40 x 14 cm (15 x 5¹/2 inch) tray lined with baking paper. Using a wet spatula, spread the mixture evenly over the tray. Freeze for 45 minutes, or until firm.
3 Preheat the oven to 220°C (425°F/ Gas 7), and lightly grease a 35 x 25 cm (14 x 9 inch) baking dish. Using a 6.5 cm (2¹/2 inch) cutter, cut the gnocchi mixture into rounds. Arrange the gnocchi in a single layer in the baking dish, and top with the remaining Parmesan. Bake for 15 minutes, or until the gnocchi are slightly puffed, then place under a hot grill (broiler) for 3 minutes, or until golden brown.
4 Put the basil, pine nuts, butter and vinegar in a pan, and mix well.
5 Arrange the tomato and gnocchi on a plate, then top with warm basil butter and serve.

NUTRITION PER SERVE
Protein 25 g; Fat 40 g; Carbohydrate 25 g; Dietary Fibre 2.5 g; Cholesterol 190 mg; 2485 kJ (595 Cal)

Slowly pour the semolina into the pan, stirring constantly.

Smooth and spread the mixture out with a wet spatula.

Use a round cutter to cut the gnocchi mixture into circles.

PUDDINGS

JAM ROLY POLY

Preparation time: 20 minutes
Total cooking time: 35 minutes
Serves 4

250 g (2 cups) self-raising flour, sifted
125 g (4¹/4 oz) butter, roughly chopped
2 tablespoons caster (superfine) sugar
50 ml (¹/4 cup) milk
210 g (²/3 cup) raspberry jam
1 tablespoon milk, extra

1 Preheat the oven to 180°C (350°F/ Gas 4) and line a baking tray with baking paper. Sift the flour into a bowl and add the butter. Using your fingertips, rub the butter into the flour until the mixture resembles fine breadcrumbs. Stir in the sugar.

2 Add the milk and 50 ml (¹/4 cup) water, and stir with a flat-bladed knife to form a dough. Turn the dough out onto a lightly floured surface and gather together.

3 On a large sheet of baking paper, roll out the dough into a thin rectangle, 33 cm (13 inches) long and 23 cm (9 inches) wide. Spread with the raspberry jam, leaving a narrow border around the edge.

4 Roll up lengthways like a Swiss roll and place on the tray seam-side down. Brush with the extra milk and cook in the oven for 35 minutes, or until golden. Leave to stand for a few minutes, then slice using a serrated knife. Serve warm with custard.

NUTRITION PER SERVE
Protein 7 g; Fat 25 g; Carbohydrate 73 g; Dietary Fibre 3 g; Cholesterol 80 mg; 2330 kJ (555 Cal)

Rub the butter into the flour with your fingertips.

Add the milk and water and mix with a flat-bladed knife to form a dough.

Roll out the dough into a rectangle on a sheet of non-stick baking paper.

Spread the jam over the dough, leaving a border around the edge.

BREAD AND BUTTER PUDDING

Preparation time: 15 minutes +
  45 minutes standing
Total cooking time: 40 minutes
Serves 4

30 g (1 oz) butter
8 thick slices day-old
  bread
2 tablespoons sultanas

3 tablespoons caster (superfine)
  sugar
1 teaspoon mixed spice
3 eggs, beaten
2 teaspoons vanilla essence
700 ml (3 cups) milk
125 ml (1/2 cup) cream
1 tablespoon demerara sugar

1 Grease a 22 x 18 x 8 cm (9 x 7 x 3 inch) ovenproof dish. Butter the bread, cut in half diagonally and layer in the dish. Sprinkle the combined sultanas, sugar and mixed spice.

2 Whisk the eggs, vanilla, milk and cream and pour over the bread. Leave to stand for 45 minutes, then top with the demerara sugar. Preheat the oven to 180°C (350°F/Gas 4).

3 Bake for about 35–40 minutes, or until the custard around the bread has set. Serve hot.

NUTRITION PER SERVE
Protein 15 g; Fat 30 g; Carbohydrate 50 g; Dietary Fibre 1.5 g; Cholesterol 220 mg; 2300 kJ (550 Cal)

Cut the bread slices in half diagonally and layer them in the prepared dish.

Slowly pour the combined eggs, vanilla, milk and cream over the bread.

Leave to soak, then scatter the demerara sugar over the top.

BAKED APPLES

Preparation time: 30 minutes
Total cooking time: 50 minutes
Serves 4

4 Granny Smith apples
50 g (1¾ oz) dried apricots,
    finely chopped
50 g (1¾ oz) dates, finely
    chopped
1 tablespoon dry breadcrumbs
½ teaspoon ground cinnamon
1 tablespoon honey, warmed
2 teaspoons apricot jam,
    warmed
20 g (½ oz) firm butter
ground nutmeg, to serve

1 Preheat the oven to 180°C (350°F/ Gas 4) and lightly grease an ovenproof dish.
2 Core the apples and, using a sharp knife, run a small slit around the circumference of each apple to stop it splitting during baking).
3 Combine the apricots, dates, breadcrumbs, cinnamon, honey and jam in a bowl. Divide the mixture into four, and push it into the apples using your fingers. Dot the top of each apple with the butter, and put the apples in the prepared dish.

4 Bake for about 45–50 minutes, or until the apples are tender all the way through—test with a skewer to be absolutely sure. Serve hot with cream or ice cream. Sprinkle some nutmeg over the top before serving.

NUTRITION PER SERVE
Protein 1 g; Fat 4 g; Carbohydrate 30 g; Dietary Fibre 4 g; Cholesterol1 13 mg; 685 kJ (165 Cal)

Carefully run a sharp knife around the circumference of each apple.

Push the mixture into each of the apples with your fingers.

APPLE CRUMBLE

Preparation time: 10 minutes
Total cooking time: 40 minutes
Serves 6

1 kg (2 lb 4 oz) green apples,
  peeled, cored and sliced
2 tablespoons caster (superfine)
  sugar
90 g (³/4 cup) plain (all-purpose)
  flour
1 teaspoon ground cinnamon
100 g (3¹/2 oz) cold butter,
  chopped
115 g (¹/2 cup) soft brown sugar
50 g (¹/2 cup) rolled oats

1 Preheat the oven to 190°C (375°F/ Gas 5). Brush a 1.25 litre (5 cup) shallow heatproof dish with melted butter. Put the apples in a bowl and add the caster sugar and 3 tablespoons water. Mix well.
2 Sift the flour and cinnamon into a bowl. With your fingertips, rub in the butter until the mixture resembles breadcrumbs. Add the brown sugar and oats, and mix well.
3 Put the apples into the dish and sprinkle on the topping. Bake for 40 minutes, or until the apples are tender and topping is golden. Sprinkle with cinnamon and serve.

NUTRITION PER SERVE
Protein 3 g; Fat 15 g; Carbohydrate 59 g; Dietary Fibre 4.5 g; Cholesterol 45 mg; 1570 kJ (375 Cal)

Carefully peel and core the apples, then cut into thin slices.

Rub in the butter, then add the brown sugar and rolled oats.

Arrange the apples over the base of the dish and sprinkle on the topping.

PECAN PIE

Preparation time: 30 minutes + chilling
Total cooking time: 1 hour 15 minutes
Serves 6

185 g (1¹/₂ cups) plain
  (all-purpose) flour
100 g (3¹/₂ oz) cold butter,
  chopped
2 tablespoons iced water

Filling
200 g (2 cups) whole pecans
3 eggs
60 g (2¹/₄ oz) butter, melted
155 g (²/₃ cup) soft brown sugar
170 ml (²/₃ cup) corn syrup
1 teaspoon vanilla essence

1 Sift the flour into a bowl then rub in the butter with your fingertips. Add the water and mix it in with a flat-bladed knife, using a cutting action, until the mixture comes together in beads. Gather the dough together, cover with plastic wrap and refrigerate for 20 minutes.
2 Transfer the dough to a sheet of baking paper and roll it out to a 3 mm (¹/₈ inch) thickness. It should be large enough to line a 23 cm (9 inch) pie dish, with some left over to decorate the edge. Invert the pastry into the dish and remove the baking paper. Line the dish with the pastry, and remove the excess. Gather the dough scraps together and roll them out to a 3 mm (¹/₈ inch) thickness. Using small cutters, cut shapes from the pastry. Brush the pastry rim with water, and attach the pastry shapes. Refrigerate for 20 minutes. Preheat the oven to 180°C (350°F/Gas 4).
3 Cover the edge of the pastry with

strips of foil to prevent burning. Line the pastry shell with a sheet of crumpled baking paper, and fill with baking beads. Bake for 15 minutes, then remove the beads and paper and bake for 15 minutes more, until the base is lightly golden. Remove the foil and cool before filling.
4 Place the pecans on the pastry base. Whisk together the eggs, butter, sugar, syrup, vanilla and a good pinch of salt. Pour over the pecans. Place the pie dish on a baking tray, and bake for 45 minutes. Cool completely.

NUTRITION PER SERVE
Protein 10 g; Fat 50 g; Carbohydrate 50 g; Dietary Fibre 4 g; Cholesterol 160 mg; 2780 kJ (665 Cal)

Invert the pastry into the pie dish, then remove the baking paper.

Use small cutters to make pastry shapes to decorate the pie edge.

Arrange the pecans evenly over the cooled pastry base.

BANANA FRITTERS

Preparation time: 20 minutes +
30 minutes standing
Total cooking time: 10 minutes
Serves 4

125 g (1 cup) self-raising flour
1 tablespoon caster (superfine)
sugar
1 teaspoon ground cinnamon
oil, for deep-frying
4 bananas

1 Sift the flour and a pinch of salt into a bowl. Make a well in the centre, and gradually add 250 ml (1 cup) water while gently whisking, drawing the flour in from the sides. The batter should be slightly lumpy—overbeating it will make it tough. Stand for 30 minutes. Combine the sugar and cinnamon in a bowl, and set aside.
2 Fill a large deep pan one third full of oil. Heat until moderately hot: when a cube of bread dropped into the oil browns in 15 seconds.
3 Cut the bananas in half crossways, slightly on the diagonal. Dip them into the batter. Drain off any excess batter and deep-fry in the hot oil for 2 minutes, or until crisp and golden. The best way to do this is to use two pairs of tongs—one to dip the bananas in the batter and lift into the oil, and one to remove from the oil. Drain on paper towels. Sprinkle with the cinnamon sugar and serve with vanilla ice cream or cream.

NUTRITION PER SERVE
Protein 3.5 g; Fat 15 g; Carbohydrate 35 g; Dietary Fibre 2 g; Cholesterol 0 mg; 1153 kJ (275 Cal)

Whisk the flour and water until the batter is just combined.

Heat the oil until a cube of bread dropped into the oil browns in 15 seconds.

Deep-fry the bananas until the batter is crisp and golden.

STICKY DATE PUDDING

Preparation time: 25 minutes +
   15 minutes standing
Total cooking time: 50 minutes
Serves 8

185 g (1 cup) chopped pitted
   dates
1 teaspoon bicarbonate of soda
90 g (3¼ oz) butter, softened
115 g (½ cup) soft brown sugar
2 eggs, lightly beaten
1 teaspoon vanilla essence
185 g (1½ cups) self-raising
   flour, sifted

Sauce
230 g (1 cup) soft brown sugar
250 ml (1 cup) cream
90 g (3¼ oz) butter
½ teaspoon vanilla essence

1 Preheat the oven to 180°C (350°F/ Gas 4). Brush an 18 cm (7 inch) square cake tin with melted butter and line the base with baking paper. Put the dates and soda in a bowl and add 250 ml (1 cup) boiling water. Stir and leave for 15 minutes.

2 Using electric beaters, beat the butter and sugar until light and creamy. Beat in the eggs gradually. Add the vanilla essence. Fold in half of the flour then half of the date mixture. Stir in the remaining flour and dates, mixing well. Pour into the prepared tin and bake for 50 minutes, or until cooked when tested with a skewer. Leave in the tin to cool for 10 minutes before turning out.

3 To make the sauce, put all ingredients in a saucepan and bring to the boil while stirring. Reduce the heat and simmer for 5 minutes. Pour over the warm pudding.

NUTRITION PER SERVE
Protein 5 g; Fat 33 g; Carbohydrate 75 g; Dietary Fibre 3 g; Cholesterol 145 mg; 2530 kJ (605 Cal)

Using a sharp knife, chop the dates into small pieces.

Pour boiling water over the dates and bicarbonate of soda.

Put the brown sugar, cream, butter and vanilla essence in a pan and simmer.

Quick-mix steamed puddings

Just saying the words "steamed pudding" conjures up a cosy fireside image. Everyone has their favourite flavour, be it traditional jam or rich banana caramel. Follow the recipe below and choose one of the flavourings from the opposite page. That's the hard part—choosing only one!

STEAMED PUDDING

1 Grease the base and side of a 1 litre (4 cup) pudding basin with melted butter. Place a round of baking paper in the bottom of the basin. Put the empty basin in a large pan on a trivet or upturned saucer and pour in enough cold water to come halfway up the sides of the basin. Remove the basin and put the water on to boil.

2 Sift 155 g (1¼ cups) self-raising flour into a bowl. Add a pinch of salt, 120 g (4½ oz) softened butter, 160 g (⅔ cup) sugar and 3 eggs and mix well. Pour into the basin.

3 Lay a sheet of foil on a work surface, cover with a sheet of baking paper, and make a large pleat in the middle. Grease the paper with melted butter. Place paper-side down across the top of the basin and tie string securely around the rim of the basin and over the top of the basin to make a handle. The string handle is used when lifting the pudding in and out of the pan.

4 Gently lower the basin into the simmering water and cover with a tight-fitting lid. Cook for 1 hour 45 minutes. Check the water level after an hour and top up to the original level with boiling water as needed. It's worth keeping a jug of water on the boil while the pudding is cooking so that the temperature (and therefore cooking time) is kept constant every time you top up. Try putting a coin in the base of the pan—it will stop rattling when the water is getting low.

Note: All variations of this recipe serve four. To reheat a steamed pudding after cooking, bring it back to room temperature and reboil for half the original cooking time. Or cut it into slices and reheat in the microwave.

From left to right: Treacle pudding; Jam pudding; Lemon pudding; Mincemeat pudding; Chocolate pudding; Banana caramel pudding

LEMON

Peel and remove the pith from a lemon. Slice the lemon and arrange slices over the base and slightly up the sides of the basin, then sprinkle with 2 teaspoons sugar. Add 1 tablespoon grated lemon zest to the pudding mixture.

NUTRITION PER SERVE
Protein 9 g; Fat 29 g; Carbohydrate 67 g; Dietary Fibre 2 g; Cholesterol 213 mg; 2310 kJ (553 Cal)

CHOCOLATE

Sift 2 tablespoons cocoa powder with the flour, and stir 90 g (1/2 cup) milk choc bits into the pudding mixture. Serve with Hot chocolate sauce (page 103).

NUTRITION PER SERVE
Protein 13 g; Fat 36 g; Carbohydrate 81 g; Dietary Fibre 2 g; Cholesterol 216 mg; 2867 kJ (685 Cal)

TREACLE

Mix 2 tablespoons treacle into the pudding mixture and place 2 teaspoons treacle in the base of the pudding bowl. When you turn the pudding out, drizzle with a little golden syrup. Serve with custard and ice cream.

NUTRITION PER SERVE
Protein 9 g; Fat 29 g; Carbohydrate 68 g; Dietary Fibre 1 g; Cholesterol 211 mg; 2431 kJ (581 Cal)

MINCEMEAT

Sift 1/4 teaspoon mixed spice with the flour, and stir 60 g (1/3 cup) fruit mince (mincemeat) into the pudding mixture. Serve with custard.

NUTRITION PER SERVE
Protein 9 g; Fat 29 g; Carbohydrate 70 g; Dietary Fibre 2 g; Cholesterol 213 mg; 2355 kJ (563 Cal)

JAM

Place 2 tablespoons strawberry jam in the base of the basin before adding the pudding mixture.

NUTRITION PER SERVE
Protein 9 g; Fat 29 g; Carbohydrate 71 g; Dietary Fibre 2 g; Cholesterol 212 mg; 2367 kJ (565 Cal)

BANANA CARAMEL

Pour 30 g (1 oz) melted butter into the pudding basin and sprinkle with 2 tablespoons soft brown sugar. Place slices of banana over the base and slightly up the sides of the pudding basin. Add 1 mashed ripe banana to the pudding mixture and mix well. Serve with freshly whipped cream.

NUTRITION PER SERVE
Protein 10 g; Fat 35 g; Carbohydrate 86 g; Dietary Fibre 3 g; Cholesterol 231 mg; 2871 kJ (686 Cal)

APPLE PIE

Preparation time: 45 minutes +
 cooling time
Total cooking time: 50 minutes
Serves 6

Filling
6 large Granny Smith apples
2 tablespoons caster (superfine)
 sugar
1 teaspoon grated lemon zest
pinch ground cloves

Pastry
250 g (2 cups) plain
 (all-purpose) flour
3 tablespoons self-raising flour
150 g (5½ oz) butter, chopped
2 tablespoons caster (superfine)
 sugar
4–5 tablespoons iced water

2 tablespoons apricot jam
1 egg, lightly beaten
1 tablespoon sugar

1 Peel, core and cut the apples into wedges. Put in a saucepan with the sugar, zest, cloves and 2 tablespoons water. Cover and cook gently for 8 minutes, or until the apples are just tender. Drain and cool.

2 Sift the flours into a bowl and add the butter. Rub the butter into the flour using your fingertips until it resembles fine crumbs. Add the sugar, mix well, then make a well in the centre. Add the water and mix with a flat-bladed knife until the mixture comes together. Gather the pastry together on a floured surface. Divide into two, making one half a little bigger. Cover with plastic wrap and refrigerate for 20 minutes.

3 Preheat the oven to 200°C (400°F/

Gas 6). Roll out the larger piece of pastry between two sheets of baking paper to line the base and side of a 23 cm (9 inch) pie plate. Peel off the top piece of paper and invert the pastry into the dish. Peel off the other baking sheet and trim the excess pastry. Brush the jam over the base and spoon the apple into the shell. Roll out the second piece of pastry between baking paper large enough to cover the pie. Brush with water around the rim, then place the top on. Trim off the excess pastry, pinch the edges together and cut a couple of steam slits in the top.

4 Gently re-roll the excess pastry bits, and cut into leaves to decorate the top. Brush the top lightly with egg then sprinkle on the sugar. Bake for 20 minutes, then reduce the oven to 180°C (350°F/Gas 4) and bake for a further 15–20 minutes, or until golden.

NUTRITION PER SERVE
Protein 6.5 g; Fat 20 g; Carbohydrate 60 g; Dietary Fibre 3.5 g; Cholesterol 95 mg; 1955 kJ (465 Cal)

Roll out the pastry between two sheets of baking paper.

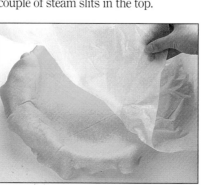

Invert the pastry into the pie dish and peel off the baking paper.

Put the pastry lid on the pie and trim off any excess pastry.

BAKED CHEESECAKE

Preparation time: 30 minutes + chilling
  and overnight refrigeration
Total cooking time: 1 hour
Serves 10

375 g (13 oz) plain sweet
  biscuits
180 g (6 oz) butter, melted

Filling
500 g (1 lb 2 oz) cream cheese
200 g (7 oz) caster (superfine)
  sugar

4 eggs
300 ml (1 carton) cream
2 tablespoons plain (all-purpose)
  flour
1 teaspoon ground cinnamon
1/4 teaspoon ground nutmeg
1 tablespoon lemon juice
2 teaspoons vanilla essence

1 Preheat the oven to 180°C (350°F/
Gas 4). Grease a 23 cm (9 inch)
shallow spring-form tin.
2 Put the biscuits in a food processor
and process until fine crumbs form.
Add the butter and process for
10 seconds. Press into the base and

sides of the tin, then refrigerate.
3 Beat the cheese and sugar together
until soft and creamy. Add the eggs
and cream and beat for about
4 minutes. Fold in the flour, cinnamon,
nutmeg, juice and vanilla essence.
Pour the mixture into the crust. Bake
for 1 hour, or until firm. Let the
cheesecake cool in the oven, turned off
with the door open. Refrigerate
overnight. Serve with cream and
strawberries.

NUTRITION PER SERVE
Protein 10 g; Fat 50 g; Carbohydrate 50 g;
Dietary Fibre 1 g; Cholesterol 215 mg;
2925 kJ (700 Cal)

*Process the biscuits in a food processor
until fine and crumbly.*

*Press the biscuit mixture into the base
and side of the tin with a spoon.*

*Pour the mixture over the biscuit base
and bake for about an hour.*

SELF-SAUCING CHOCOLATE PUDDING

Preparation time: 10 minutes
Total cooking time: 45 minutes
Serves 6

125 g (1 cup) self-raising flour
3 tablespoons cocoa powder
125 g (½ cup) caster (superfine)
　sugar
1 egg
125 ml (½ cup) milk
60 g (2¼ oz) butter,
　melted

1 teaspoon vanilla essence
185 g (1 cup) soft brown sugar

1 Preheat the oven to 180°C (350°F/ Gas 4). Brush a 2 litre (8 cup) heatproof dish with melted butter. Sift the flour and 1 tablespoon cocoa into a large bowl and add the sugar. Make a well in the mixture.
2 In a jug, beat the egg and add the milk, melted butter and vanilla essence. Pour the liquid into the dry ingredients and, using a wooden spoon, stir the batter until well combined and lump free. Pour into the prepared dish.

3 Combine the brown sugar and the remaining cocoa and sprinkle evenly over the batter. Pour 375 ml (1½ cups) boiling water gently and evenly over the ingredients in the dish. Bake for 30–40 minutes, or until the pudding is cooked—a sauce will have formed underneath. Serve hot with whipped cream or ice cream.

NUTRITION PER SERVE
Protein 6 g; Fat 11 g; Carbohydrate 70 g; Dietary Fibre 1 g; Cholesterol 60 mg; 1640 kJ (390 Cal)

Add the egg mixture to the dry ingredients and stir with a wooden spoon.

Sprinkle the combined sugar and cocoa over the batter.

Gently pour the boiling water evenly over the pudding.

TRIFLE

Preparation time: 15 minutes
Total cooking time: 10 minutes
Serves 6

45 g (½ cup) flaked almonds
250 g (9 oz) packet jam rollettes
　(mini jam Swiss rolls)
80 ml (⅓ cup) medium dry
　sherry
2 fresh mangoes or 2 fresh
　peaches, chopped

600 ml (2½ cups) ready-made
　custard
300 ml (1 carton) cream

1 Preheat the oven to 180°C (350°F/ Gas 4). Scatter the flaked almonds over a baking tray and cook in the oven for 6–8 minutes, or until golden. Cut the jam rollettes into thin slices and place half on the base of a 2.5 litre (10 cup) glass serving bowl.
2 Pour over half the sherry and add half the chopped mango or peach. Cover with half the custard. Repeat

layering with the remaining ingredients, then refrigerate until trifle is cold.
3 Whisk the cream until stiff peaks form, then spread over the custard and scatter with the toasted almonds. Serve immediately.

NUTRITION PER SERVE
Protein 9 g; Fat 27 g; Carbohydrate 45 g; Dietary Fibre 1.5 g; Cholesterol 130 mg; 1920 kJ (460 Cal)

Scatter the almonds on a baking tray and cook until golden.

Sprinkle the sherry over the jam rollettes then add the fruit.

Whip the cream until stiff peaks form, then spread it over the custard.

Self-saucing chocolate pudding (top) and Trifle

CREAMY CHOCOLATE MOUSSE

Preparation time: 5 minutes +
  overnight chilling
Total cooking time: 5 minutes
Serves 6

125 g (4¹/2 oz) dark chocolate,
  chopped
4 eggs, separated
185 ml (³/4 cup) cream, whipped

1 Put the chocolate in a heatproof bowl. Bring a pan of water to a simmer, remove from the heat and place the bowl over the pan (don't let the base of the bowl touch the water). Melt the chocolate, stirring occasionally. Remove from the heat and cool slightly. Lightly beat the egg yolks and stir into the chocolate mixture. Fold in the cream.

2 Using electric beaters, whisk the egg whites in a small bowl until soft peaks form. Fold one spoonful of the egg whites into the mousse with a metal spoon, then gently fold in the remainder, quickly and lightly.

3 Pour the mousse into six wine glasses or 185 ml (³/4 cup) ramekins. Cover with plastic wrap and refrigerate for 4 hours or overnight. Top with extra whipped cream and dust with cocoa powder, if desired.

NUTRITION PER SERVE
Protein 6 g; Fat 22 g; Carbohydrate 15 g; Dietary Fibre 0 g; Cholesterol 160 mg; 1150 kJ (275 Cal)

Put the bowl of chocolate over a pan of simmering water and stir occasionally.

Fold the egg whites into the mousse with a metal spoon.

Pour the mousse into wine glasses or ramekins before covering and chilling.

CARAMEL BANANAS

Preparation time: 5 minutes
Total cooking time: 10 minutes
Serves 4

60 g (2¼ oz) butter
100 g (3½ oz) soft brown sugar
2 tablespoons lemon juice
1 tablespoon orange liqueur
4 firm, ripe bananas, sliced in
   half lengthways

1 Melt the butter in a large frying pan. Add the sugar and stir to combine, then simmer for 3 minutes, or until golden and bubbly.
2 Add the lemon juice and liqueur, and stir gently. Put the bananas in the sauce and simmer for 5 minutes, or until the sauce thickens. Occasionally spoon the sauce over the bananas to baste them. The caramel bananas are delicious served with good-quality vanilla ice cream or with waffles and whipped cream.

NUTRITION PER SERVE
Protein 0 g; Fat 10 g; Carbohydrate 28 g; Dietary Fibre 0 g; Cholesterol 38 mg; 950 kJ (225 Cal)

COOK'S FILE

Variation: This recipe also makes a delicious pancake filling if you chop the bananas instead of halving them.

Add the brown sugar to the pan when the butter has melted.

Put the bananas in the pan when the caramel is golden and bubbly.

Spoon the caramel sauce over the bananas to baste them.

PANCAKES WITH HOT CHOCOLATE SAUCE

Preparation time: 5 minutes +
  30 minutes standing
Total cooking time: 20 minutes
Makes 12 pancakes

250 g (2 cups) plain
  (all-purpose) flour
3 eggs, lightly beaten
250 ml (1 cup) milk
60 g (2^1/$_4$ oz) butter, melted

Sauce
2 tablespoons butter
3 tablespoons sifted cocoa powder
185 g (1 cup) soft brown sugar
300 ml (10^1/$_2$ fl oz) carton cream

1 Sift the flour into a large bowl. Make a well in the centre and add the combined eggs, milk and 185 ml (^{3}/$_4$ cup) water. With a whisk gradually draw in the flour and whisk to a smooth batter. Stir in the melted butter. Pour into a jug and set aside for 30 minutes.

2 Heat a 20 cm (8 inch) crepe pan or non-stick frying pan and grease lightly with butter. When the pan is hot, pour in 60 ml (^{1}/$_4$ cup) of the mixture and tilt the pan to cover. Tip out any excess batter. When the edges begin to curl, gently turn the pancake over with a spatula. Cook until lightly browned on both sides, and slide onto a plate. If serving immediately, keep the pancakes warm. Cook the remaining batter and stack the pancakes on top of each other as you go with a piece of greaseproof paper between each one.

3 To make the sauce, combine in a pan the butter, cocoa and sugar. Mix well, then add the cream and stir over low heat until the mixture comes to the boil.

4 To serve, fold three pancakes into quarters and put them on a plate. Pour a generous amount of the sauce over the top and add a scoop of vanilla ice cream.

NUTRITION PER PANCAKE
Protein 6 g; Fat 20 g; Carbohydrate 33 g; Dietary Fibre 1 g; Cholesterol 100 mg; 1395 kJ (335 Cal)

Whisk together the flour, eggs, milk and water and stir in the melted butter.

Pour the mixture into the hot pan and tilt to cover the base.

When the edges begin to curl, gently turn the pancake over.

Cook the pancake until lightly browned on both sides.

LEMON DELICIOUS

Preparation time: 10 minutes
Total cooking time: 45 minutes
Serves 4

30 g (1 oz) butter, softened
185 g ($^3/4$ cup) caster
   (superfine) sugar
1 teaspoon grated lemon zest
3 eggs, separated
30 g ($^1/4$ cup) plain (all-purpose)
   flour
125 ml ($^1/2$ cup) lemon juice

375 ml (1$^1/2$ cups) warm milk
icing (confectioners') sugar,
   to dust

1 Preheat the oven to 180°C (350°F/ Gas 4). Brush a 1.5 litre (6 cup) heatproof dish with melted butter. Put the butter, sugar, zest and yolks in a bowl. Using electric beaters, beat until light and creamy.
2 Fold in the sifted flour in two batches, alternately with the lemon juice and milk. In a separate clean dry bowl, using electric beaters, whisk the egg whites until soft peaks form.

Pour the lemon mixture down the inside of the bowl of beaten egg whites and fold the whites gently into the mixture.
3 Pour the mixture into the prepared dish and put the dish in a baking tin. Pour in enough warm water to come halfway up the sides of the dish. Bake for 40 minutes, or until golden. Dust with icing sugar and serve with ice cream.

NUTRITION PER SERVE
Protein 9 g; Fat 15 g; Carbohydrate 60 g; Dietary Fibre 0 g; Cholesterol 165 mg; 1630 kJ (390 Cal)

Fold in the flour alternately with the lemon juice and milk.

Pour the lemon mixture down the inside of the bowl of beaten egg whites.

Gently fold the egg whites into the mixture with a spoon.

HOT CHOCOLATE SOUFFLE

Preparation time: 10 minutes
Total cooking time: 35 minutes
Serves 8

170 g (6 oz) caster (superfine) sugar
450 ml (16 fl oz) milk
70 g (2¹/₂ oz) plain (all-purpose) flour
1 egg
4 eggs, separated
40 g (1¹/₂ oz) butter, melted
30 g (¹/₄ cup) cocoa powder, sifted

1 tablespoon caster (superfine) sugar, extra

1 Grease a 1.25 litre (5 cup) soufflé dish and preheat the oven to 200°C (400 °F/Gas 6).

2 Put the sugar and 250 ml (1 cup) milk in a pan and stir over low heat until the sugar dissolves. Put the flour, egg and remaining milk in a bowl and whisk to combine. Pour the mixture into the bowl and mix well. When smooth, return the mixture to the pan and stir over low heat until it boils and thickens. Combine the yolks and butter with the cocoa and add to the pan, mixing well. Put in a bowl, cover, and leave to cool.

3 In a large clean dry bowl, beat the egg whites until soft peaks form, then add the extra sugar. Continue beating until the egg whites are glossy. Carefully combine one spoonful of the egg whites with the chocolate mixture, then add the remaining egg white and fold in gently with a metal spoon.

4 Fill the soufflé dish to three-quarters full and put on an oven tray. Cook in the oven for 25–30 minutes, or until puffed up and firm. Dust with icing sugar before serving.

NUTRITION PER SERVE
Protein 7.5 g; Fat 10 g; Carbohydrate 35 g; Dietary Fibre 0.5 g; Cholesterol 135 mg; 1065 kJ (255 Cal)

Whisk or stir over low heat until the mixture thickens and comes to the boil.

Gently fold the egg whites into the chocolate mixture with a metal spoon.

Pour the mixture into the prepared dish to three-quarters full.

BAKED CUSTARD

Preparation time: 5 minutes
Total cooking time: 35 minutes
Serves 4

3 eggs
2 tablespoons caster (superfine) sugar
1 teaspoon vanilla essence
500 ml (2 cups) milk
125 ml (¹/₂ cup) cream
ground nutmeg, to sprinkle

1 Preheat the oven to 160°C (315°F/ Gas 2–3). Brush a 1.5 litre (6 cup) heatproof dish with a little melted butter. Put the eggs, sugar and vanilla essence in a bowl and whisk lightly to combine. (If you overwhisk you may have bubbles in your finished custard.) Heat the milk and cream together in a pan until just warm and then stir into the eggs, mixing well.

2 Strain the mixture into the prepared dish and sprinkle with a little nutmeg. Put the dish in a baking tin and pour enough hot water in the tin to come halfway up the side of the custard dish.

3 Bake for 35 minutes, or until the custard is set—it shouldn't wobble in the centre when shaken. Remove immediately from the baking tin. Serve the custard warm or at room temperature.

NUTRITION PER SERVE
Protein 9.5 g; Fat 22 g; Carbohydrate 17 g; Dietary Fibre 0 g; Cholesterol 195 mg; 1245 kJ (295 Cal)

COOK'S FILE

Variations: To make a brandied raisin custard, soak 3 tablespoons of chopped raisins in 2 tablespoons of brandy for 30 minutes. Discard the brandy, and add the raisins to the custard mixture.

Strain the warm custard mixture into the prepared dish.

Pour hot water into the baking tin to come halfway up the side of the custard dish.

Hot chocolate soufflé (top) and Baked custard

PLUM COBBLER

Preparation time: 25 minutes
Total cooking time: 35 minutes
Serves 6

750 g (1 lb 10 oz) plums
90 g (1/3 cup) sugar
1 teaspoon vanilla essence

Topping
125 g (1 cup) self-raising flour
60 g (2¼ oz) butter, chopped
55 g (¼ cup) soft brown sugar
60 ml (¼ cup) milk
1 tablespoon caster (superfine)
   sugar

1 Preheat the oven to 200°C (400°F/ Gas 6). Cut the plums into quarters and remove the stones. Put the plums, sugar and 2 tablespoons water into a pan and bring to the boil, stirring, until the sugar dissolves.

2 Reduce the heat, then cover and simmer for 5 minutes, or until the plums are tender. Add the vanilla essence and spoon the mixture into a 750 ml (3 cup) ovenproof dish.

3 To make the topping, sift the flour into a bowl and add the butter. Using your fingertips, rub the butter into the flour until it resembles fine breadcrumbs. Stir in the brown sugar and 2 tablespoons milk.

4 Stir with a knife to form a soft dough, adding more milk if required. Turn the mixture out onto a lightly floured surface and knead to form a smooth dough. Roll out the dough to an even thickness and cut into rounds with a 4 cm (1½ inch) cutter.

5 Overlap the rounds around the side of the dish over the filling. (The plums in the middle will not be covered.) Lightly brush with milk and sprinkle with sugar. Cook in the oven on a baking tray for 30 minutes, or until golden.

NUTRITION PER SERVE
Protein 3 g; Fat 9 g; Carbohydrate 50 g; Dietary Fibre 3.5 g; Cholesterol 25 mg; 1245 kJ (295 Cal)

Sift the flour into a bowl, then rub in the butter with your fingertips.

Stir with a flat-bladed knife to form a soft dough.

Brush the tin with melted butter and sprinkle brown sugar over the base.

Put the pineapple rings on the butter and sugar at the base of the tin.

Fold in the flours, coconut and pineapple juice with a metal spoon.

Spoon in the mixture and indent the centre slightly with the back of a spoon.

PINEAPPLE UPSIDE-DOWN CAKE

Preparation time: 30 minutes
Total cooking time: 1 hour
Serves 6

90 g (3¼ oz) butter, melted
95 g (½ cup) soft brown sugar
440 g (1 lb) can pineapple rings
6 glacé cherries
125 g (4½ oz) butter, chopped
185 g (¾ cup) caster
    (superfine) sugar
2 eggs
1 teaspoon vanilla essence
185 g (1½ cups) self-raising
    flour
60 g (½ cup) plain (all-purpose)
    flour
30 g (⅓ cup) desiccated coconut

1 Preheat the oven to 180°C (350°F/ Gas 4). Pour the melted butter into a 20 cm (8 inch) round tin, brushing some of it up the side, but leaving most on the base. Sprinkle the brown sugar over the base. Drain the pineapple, reserving 125 ml (½ cup) of the juice. Arrange the pineapple rings over the base of the tin and put a cherry in the centre of each ring.

2 Using electric beaters, beat the butter and the sugar until light and creamy. Add the eggs one at a time, beating well each time. Add the vanilla and beat until combined.

3 Sift the flours into the butter mixture, then add the coconut and reserved juice. Fold in with a metal spoon until just combined. Spoon the mixture into the tin over the pineapple and smooth the surface. Indent the centre slightly with the back of a spoon to ensure the cake has a reasonably flat base.

4 Bake for 50–60 minutes, or until golden. Leave the cake in the tin for 10 minutes before turning out.

NUTRITION PER SERVE
Protein 7 g; Fat 35 g; Carbohydrate 84 g; Dietary Fibre 3 g; Cholesterol 152 mg; 2777 kJ (663 Cal)

Sweet sauces

When your sweet tooth is crying out for attention, look no further than these fabulous recipes for sweet sauces. From almost healthy fruity sauces to classic hot chocolate sauce, there is a topping to suit everyone. Enjoy them on their own or poured over ice cream, steamed puddings, baked cheesecakes, pancakes, waffles—the list is endless—and indulge yourself.

RHUBARB SAUCE

Chop 350 g (12 oz) rhubarb and place in a pan with 95 g (1/2 cup) soft brown sugar, 250 ml (1 cup) water and 1/4 teaspoon ground mixed spice. Slowly bring to the boil, stirring to dissolve the sugar. Simmer for 10 minutes, stirring often. Push through a sieve and serve hot or cold with warm orange or butter cake. Serves 6.

NUTRITION PER SERVE
Protein 1 g; Fat 0 g; Carbohydrate 17 g; Dietary Fibre 2 g; Cholesterol 0 mg; 290 kJ (69 Cal)

BUTTERSCOTCH SAUCE

Put 125 g (4½ oz) butter and 90 g (3¼ oz) soft brown sugar in a pan and stir over low heat until the butter has melted and the sugar has dissolved. Bring to the boil, then add 2 tablespoons golden syrup and 125 ml (1/2 cup) cream. Reduce the heat and simmer for 10 minutes. Serve with sticky date pudding. Serves 6.

NUTRITION PER SERVE
Protein 1 g; Fat 26 g; Carbohydrate 23 g; Dietary Fibre 0 g; Cholesterol 82 mg; 1330 kJ (318 Cal)

From left to right:
Hot chocolate sauce; Crème Anglaise; Butterscotch sauce;
Hot blueberry sauce; Rhubarb sauce; Vanilla custard

CREME ANGLAISE

Put 3 egg yolks into a bowl with 2 tablespoons caster (superfine) sugar and beat with a balloon whisk until light and fluffy. Heat 375 ml (1½ cups) milk in a pan and bring it to scalding point, then pour into the egg mixture, stirring with the whisk until well combined. Return to a clean pan and heat over low heat, stirring constantly to ensure it thickens evenly. Do not let the custard boil or it will curdle. It is ready when you can draw a line through it which will hold its shape. Stir through 1 teaspoon vanilla essence. Serve with pudding or fresh fruit. Serves 6–8.

NUTRITION PER SERVE (8)
Protein 3 g; Fat 4 g; Carbohydrate 7 g; Dietary Fibre 0 g; Cholesterol 73 mg; 295 kJ (71 Cal)

HOT CHOCOLATE SAUCE

Place 250 g (9 oz) chopped dark chocolate in a pan with 185 ml (¾ cup) cream, 50 g (1¾ oz) butter and 1 tablespoon golden syrup. Stir over low heat until the chocolate melts and the mixture is smooth. Serve with poached pears and cream. Serves 6.

NUTRITION PER SERVE
Protein 3 g; Fat 32 g; Carbohydrate 27 g; Dietary Fibre 0 g; Cholesterol 63 mg; 1662 kJ (397 Cal)

VANILLA CUSTARD

Place 250 ml (1 cup) milk and 250 ml (1 cup) cream in a pan, stir to combine and bring to the boil. Remove from the heat. Whisk together 3 egg yolks, 90 g (⅓ cup) caster (superfine) sugar and 2 teaspoons cornflour (cornstarch) in a heatproof bowl. Slowly add the hot milk mixture, whisking continuously, then return the mixture to the pan and stir over low heat until the custard thickens. Remove from the heat and add 1 teaspoon vanilla essence. Serve with pancakes and berries. Serves 6–8.

NUTRITION PER SERVE (8)
Protein 3 g; Fat 16 g; Carbohydrate 14 g; Dietary Fibre 0 g; Cholesterol 114 mg; 880 kJ (210 Cal)

HOT BLUEBERRY SAUCE

Combine 500 g (1 lb 2 oz) blueberries and 2 tablespoons balsamic vinegar in a non-metallic bowl, and leave for 30 minutes to macerate the fruit. Place in a pan with 60 g (¼ cup) caster (superfine) sugar and cook, stirring, over low heat to dissolve the sugar. Bring to the boil and simmer for 2–3 minutes. Serve warm with ice cream or pancakes. Serves 6.

NUTRITION PER SERVE
Protein 1 g; Fat 0 g; Carbohydrate 19 g; Dietary Fibre 2 g; Cholesterol 0 mg; 333 kJ (79 Cal)

TIRAMISU

Preparation time: 20 minutes +
  overnight chilling
Total cooking time: Nil
Serves 8

375 ml (1½ cups) strongly
  brewed espresso coffee
185 ml (¾ cup) Kahlua or
  Tia Maria
500 g (1 lb 2 oz) mascarpone
2 tablespoons caster (superfine)
  sugar
125 ml (½ cup) cream, lightly
  whipped
260 g (9 oz) thin sponge finger
  biscuits
30 g (¼ cup) cocoa powder

1 Combine the coffee and 125 ml
(½ cup) of Kahlua or Tia Maria and
set aside in a shallow dish.
2 Mix the mascarpone, sugar and
remaining Kahlua or Tia Maria in a
large bowl until well combined, then
gently fold in the cream. Cover and
refrigerate.
3 Dip half the sponge finger biscuits
into the coffee mixture (it is important
to do this quickly so they do not take
up too much liquid and go soggy), and
place them in a single layer on the
bottom of a 2 litre (8 cup) ceramic
dish.
4 Spread half of the mascarpone
mixture over the biscuits and dust
liberally with half of the cocoa, using
a fine sieve. Dunk the remaining
biscuits in the coffee and lay them on
top, then spread with the remaining
mascarpone. Dust with the remaining
cocoa, then cover and refrigerate
overnight to allow the flavours to
develop.

NUTRITION PER SERVE
Protein 9 g; Fat 26 g; Carbohydrate 64 g;
Dietary Fibre 1 g; Cholesterol 82 mg;
2142 kJ (512 Cal)

COOK'S FILE

Note: Tiramisu means 'pick-me-up'
in Italian. Sometimes referred to as
Italian trifle, tiramisu actually has a
much lighter texture than trifle.
Variation: If you would prefer this
as an alcohol-free dessert, you can
omit the Kahlua or Tia Maria and us e
185 ml (¾ cup) more coffee instead.

*Mix together the mascarpone, sugar and
remaining Kahlua or Tia Maria.*

*Quickly dip half the biscuits in the coffee
mixture and layer in the base of the dish.*

*Spoon half of the mascarpone mixture
over the biscuits.*

*Dust the top layer of the mascarpone
mixture with finely sifted cocoa.*

SPICED APPLE SPONGE

Preparation time: 15 minutes
Total cooking time: 45 minutes
Serves 4

**850 g (1 lb 14 oz) Granny Smith
    apples**
30 g (1 oz) butter
40 g (¹/3 cup) raisins
2 tablespoons lemon juice
4 cloves
1 cinnamon stick
pinch nutmeg
**160 g (²/3 cup) caster
    (superfine) sugar**
2 eggs
finely grated zest of 1 lemon
30 g (¹/4 cup) self-raising flour

**30 g (¹/4 cup) cornflour
    (cornstarch)**
**sifted icing (confectioners')
    sugar, to serve**

1 Preheat the oven to 180°C (350°F/
Gas 4). Peel, core and slice the apples
into eighths. Melt the butter in a frying
pan, add the apples and cook, stirring
occasionally, over high heat for
7 minutes, or until browned. Add the
raisins, juice, cloves, cinnamon,
nutmeg, half the sugar and 125 ml
(¹/2 cup) water. Bring to the boil, then
lower the heat and simmer for
3 minutes, or until the apples are
tender. Remove the cinnamon stick
and cloves. Spoon the apple mixture
into a deep 2 litre (8 cup) round
ovenproof dish.

2 To make the sponge topping, beat
the eggs, remaining sugar and lemon
zest in a small bowl with electric
beaters for 7–8 minutes, or until the
mixture is light and creamy. Fold in
the sifted flours with a metal spoon.
3 Spoon the sponge topping over
the apples. Bake in the oven for
30 minutes, or until the sponge is
well risen and golden. Dust with
icing sugar before serving. Suggested
accompaniments include ice cream,
whipped cream, hot or cold custard,
sweetened ricotta cheese, and spiced
mascarpone.

NUTRITION PER SERVE
Protein 5.5 g; Fat 9 g; Carbohydrate 88 g;
Dietary Fibre 5 g; Cholesterol 105 mg;
1833 kJ (438 Cal)

*Add the apples to the pan and cook until
well browned.*

*Remove the cloves and cinnamon stick
when the apples are tender.*

*Spread the sponge topping evenly over
the apples before baking.*

RICE PUDDING

Preparation time: 10 minutes
Total cooking time: 2 hours
Serves 4

55 g (1/4 cup) short-grain rice
410 ml (1²/3 cups) milk
1¹/2 tablespoons caster
(superfine) sugar
185 ml (³/4 cup) cream

1/4 teaspoon vanilla essence
1/4 teaspoon grated nutmeg
1 bay leaf

1 Preheat the oven to 150°C (300°F/ Gas 2) and grease a 1 litre (4 cup) ovenproof dish. In a bowl, mix together the rice, milk, caster sugar, cream and vanilla essence, and pour into the prepared dish. Dust the surface of the pudding with the grated nutmeg and float the bay leaf on top.

2 Bake the rice pudding for 2 hours, by which time the rice should have absorbed most of the milk and will have become creamy in texture with a brown skin on top. Serve hot.

NUTRITION PER SERVE
Protein 5 g; Fat 24 g; Carbohydrate 25 g; Dietary Fibre 0 g; Cholesterol 77 mg; 1378 kJ (330 Cal)

Mix together the rice, milk, caster sugar, cream and vanilla essence.

Pour the mixture into a greased ovenproof dish and dust with nutmeg.

Float the bay leaf on the top to allow its flavours to infuse.

LEMON MERINGUE PIE

Preparation time: 1 hour + chilling
Total cooking time: 45 minutes
Serves 6

185 g (1½ cups) plain
    (all-purpose) flour
2 tablespoons icing
    (confectioners') sugar
125 g (4½ oz) cold butter,
    chopped
2–3 tablespoons iced water

Filling
30 g (¼ cup) cornflour
    (cornstarch)
30 g (¼ cup) plain (all-purpose)
    flour
250 g (1 cup) caster (superfine)
    sugar
185 ml (¾ cup) lemon juice
3 teaspoons grated lemon zest
40 g (1½ oz) butter
6 eggs, separated
375 g (1½ cups) caster
    (superfine) sugar, extra
½ teaspoon cornflour
    (cornstarch), extra

1 Sift the flour into a bowl and add the icing sugar and butter. Using your fingertips, rub in the butter. Add 2 tablespoons water and mix into the flour with a flat-bladed knife until the mixture comes together. Add the remaining water if required.
2 Put the dough on a sheet of baking paper and roll out to fit a greased 23 cm (9 inch) round pie dish. Ease the pastry into the dish. Trim excess pastry and pinch or fork the edge. Refrigerate for 15 minutes.
3 Preheat the oven to 180°C (350°F/ Gas 4). Place a sheet of baking paper

in the pie shell and spread a layer of baking beads over the top. Bake for 10–15 minutes, then remove the paper and beads, and bake for a further 10 minutes. Remove from the oven and cool.
4 To make the filling, put the flours and sugar in a pan. Whisk in the juice, rind and 375 ml (1½ cups) water. Whisk over medium heat until the mixture boils and thickens, then reduce the heat and cook for 1 minute. Remove from the heat and whisk in the butter and yolks, one at a time. Cover and set aside to cool.

5 Preheat the oven to 220°C (425°F/ Gas 7). Spread the filling into the pastry shell. Put the egg whites and extra sugar in a mixing bowl. Beat with electric beaters on high for 10 minutes, or until the sugar is dissolved and the meringue is glossy. Beat in the cornflour. Spread the meringue over the top of the pie, and bake for 5–10 minutes, or until golden. Cool before serving.

NUTRITION PER SERVE
Protein 4 g; Fat 18 g; Carbohydrate 80 g; Dietary Fibre 1.5 g; Cholesterol 53 mg; 2020 kJ (483 Cal)

Remove the paper, beans or rice and bake until the pastry is cooked through.

Whisk the lemon mixture over medium heat until it boils and thickens.

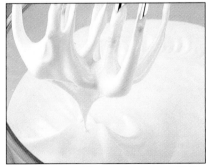

Beat the egg whites and sugar until the meringue is thick and glossy.

GRANDMOTHER'S PAVLOVA

Preparation time: 30 minutes
Total cooking time: 1 hour
Serves 6

4 egg whites
1 cup (250 g) caster (superfine)
    sugar
2 teaspoons cornflour
    (cornstarch)
1 teaspoon white vinegar
500 ml (2 cups) cream
3 passionfruit
strawberries, for decoration

1 Preheat the oven to 160°C (315°F/ Gas 2–3). Line a 32 x 28 cm (12 x 11 inch) baking tray with baking paper.
2 Put the egg whites and a pinch of salt in a small bowl. Using electric beaters, beat until stiff peaks form. Add the sugar gradually, beating constantly, until the sugar has dissolved and the mixture is glossy.
3 Using a metal spoon, fold in the cornflour and vinegar. Spoon the mixture into a mound on the baking tray. Lightly flatten the top of the pavlova and smooth the sides. Bake for 1 hour, or until pale cream and crisp. Remove from the oven while warm and carefully turn upside down onto a plate. Allow to cool.
4 Lightly whip the cream until soft peaks form, and spread over the centre. Decorate with passionfruit pulp and strawberry halves.

NUTRITION PER SERVE
Protein 4 g; Fat 36 g; Carbohydrate 45 g; Dietary Fibre 1.5 g; Cholesterol 113 mg; 2124 kJ (507 Cal)

Beat until the mixture is thick and glossy and all the sugar has dissolved.

Spoon the mixture onto the baking tray with a metal spoon.

Smooth the top and sides to give the pavlova a cake shape.

GOLDEN SYRUP DUMPLINGS

Preparation time: 15 minutes
Total cooking time: 30 minutes
Serves 4

**125 g (1 cup) self-raising flour
40 g (1½ oz) cold butter,
    chopped
1 egg
1 tablespoon milk
250 g (1 cup) sugar**

**40 g (1½ oz) butter, extra
2 tablespoons golden syrup
60 ml (¼ cup) lemon juice**

1 Sift the flour into a bowl with a pinch of salt. Using your fingertips, rub the butter into the flour until it resembles fine crumbs. Make a well in the centre. Using a flat-bladed knife, stir the combined egg and milk into the flour to form a soft dough.
2 To make the syrup, place 500 ml (2 cups) water in a large pan with the sugar, butter, golden syrup and lemon juice. Stir over medium heat until the sugar has dissolved.
3 Bring to the boil, then gently drop dessertspoons of the dough into the syrup. Reduce the heat to a simmer and cook, covered, for 20 minutes, or until a knife inserted into a dumpling comes out clean. Spoon onto serving plates, drizzle with syrup, and serve immediately.

NUTRITION PER SERVE
Protein 5 g; Fat 20 g; Carbohydrate 95 g; Dietary Fibre 1 g; Cholesterol 97 mg; 2327 kJ (555 Cal)

Rub the butter into the flour until the mixture resembles breadcrumbs.

Stir the milk and egg into the flour mixture with a flat-bladed knife.

Carefully drop dessertspoons of dough into the boiling syrup.

SPOTTED DICK

Preparation time: 20 minutes
Total cooking time: 1 hour 30 minutes
Serves 4

185 g (1½ cups) plain
   (all-purpose) flour
1½ teaspoons baking powder
125 g (½ cup) sugar
1½ teaspoons ground ginger
160 g (2 cups) fresh
   breadcrumbs
60 g (2¼ oz) sultanas
110 g (4 oz) currants
125 g (1½ cups) grated suet
2 teaspoons finely grated
   lemon zest
2 eggs, lightly beaten
170 ml (²/3 cup) milk

1 Sift the flour, baking powder, sugar and ginger into a large bowl. Add the breadcrumbs, sultanas, currants, suet and lemon zest. Mix thoroughly with a wooden spoon.

2 Combine the egg and milk, and add to the dry ingredients. Mix together well, adding a little more milk if necessary, then set aside for 5 minutes. Lay a sheet of baking paper on the work surface and form the mixture into a roll shape about 20 cm (8 inches) long. Roll the pudding in the paper and fold up the ends (do not wrap it too tight as it has to expand as it cooks). Wrap the roll in a tea towel, put it in the top of a bamboo steamer over a wok filled one third full of water. Cover and allow to simmer for 1½ hours. Do not let the pudding boil dry—replenish with boiling water as the pudding cooks. Unmould the pudding onto a serving plate, cut into slices and serve with warm custard or cream.

NUTRITION PER SERVE
Protein 16 g; Fat 33 g; Carbohydrate 110 g; Dietary Fibre 5 g; Cholesterol 120 mg; 3337 kJ (795 Cal)

COOK'S FILE

Note: Suet can be bought at good butchers, but as they might have to get it in specially, order it a few days before you need it. Store suet in the freezer until ready to use—this makes it much easier to grate.

Grate the suet with the rough side of a cheese grater.

Mix together the milk and eggs and add to the dry ingredients.

Form the mixture into a roll shape and roll it up in baking paper.

Wrap the pudding in a clean tea towel and steam in the top of a steamer.

INDEX

INTERNATIONAL GLOSSARY OF INGREDIENTS

capsicum	red or green pepper	fresh coriander	fresh cilantro
eggplant	aubergine	English spinach	spinach
zucchini	courgette	jaffle	toasted sandwich
tomato paste (Aus.)	tomato purée, double concentrate (UK)	tomato purée (Aus.)	sieved crushed tomatoes/ passata (UK)

This edition published in 2008 by Bay Books, an imprint of Murdoch Books Pty Limited. Pier 8/9, 23 Hickson Road, Millers Point, NSW 2000, Australia

Editor: Zoë Harpham **Designers:** Annette Fitzgerald, Wing Ping Tong **Food Director:** Jody Vassallo. **Food Editors:** Rebecca Clancy, Lulu Grimes **Recipe Development:** Anna Beaumont, Janene Brooks, Michelle Earl, Lulu Grimes, Kathy Knudsen, Barbara Lowery, Sally Parker, Justine Poole, Jo Richardson, Tracy Rutherford, Dimitra Stais, Jody Vassallo **Home Economists:** Alison Adams, Anna Beaumont, Michelle Lawton, Beth Michell, Kate Murdoch, Justine Poole, Margot Smithyman **Nutritionist:** Thérèse Abbey **Photographers:** Tony Lyon, Reg Morrison (steps), Chris Jones **Food Stylists:** Michelle Noerianto , Maria Villegas (cover), Mary Harris **Food Preparation:** Kerrie Mullins, Michelle Lawton
Chief Executive: Juliet Rogers **Publisher:** Kay Scarlett

The nutritional information provided for each recipe does not include garnishes or accompaniments, such as rice, unless they are included in specific quantities in the ingredients. The values are approximations and can be affected by biological and seasonal variations in food, the unknown composition of some manufactured foods and uncertainty in the dietary database. Nutrient data given are derived primarily from the NUTTAB95 database produced by the Australian New Zealand Food Authority.

ISBN 978 0 681 24495 5
Printed by Sing Cheong Printing Co. Ltd. PRINTED IN CHINA.